Grimm's Fairy Stories

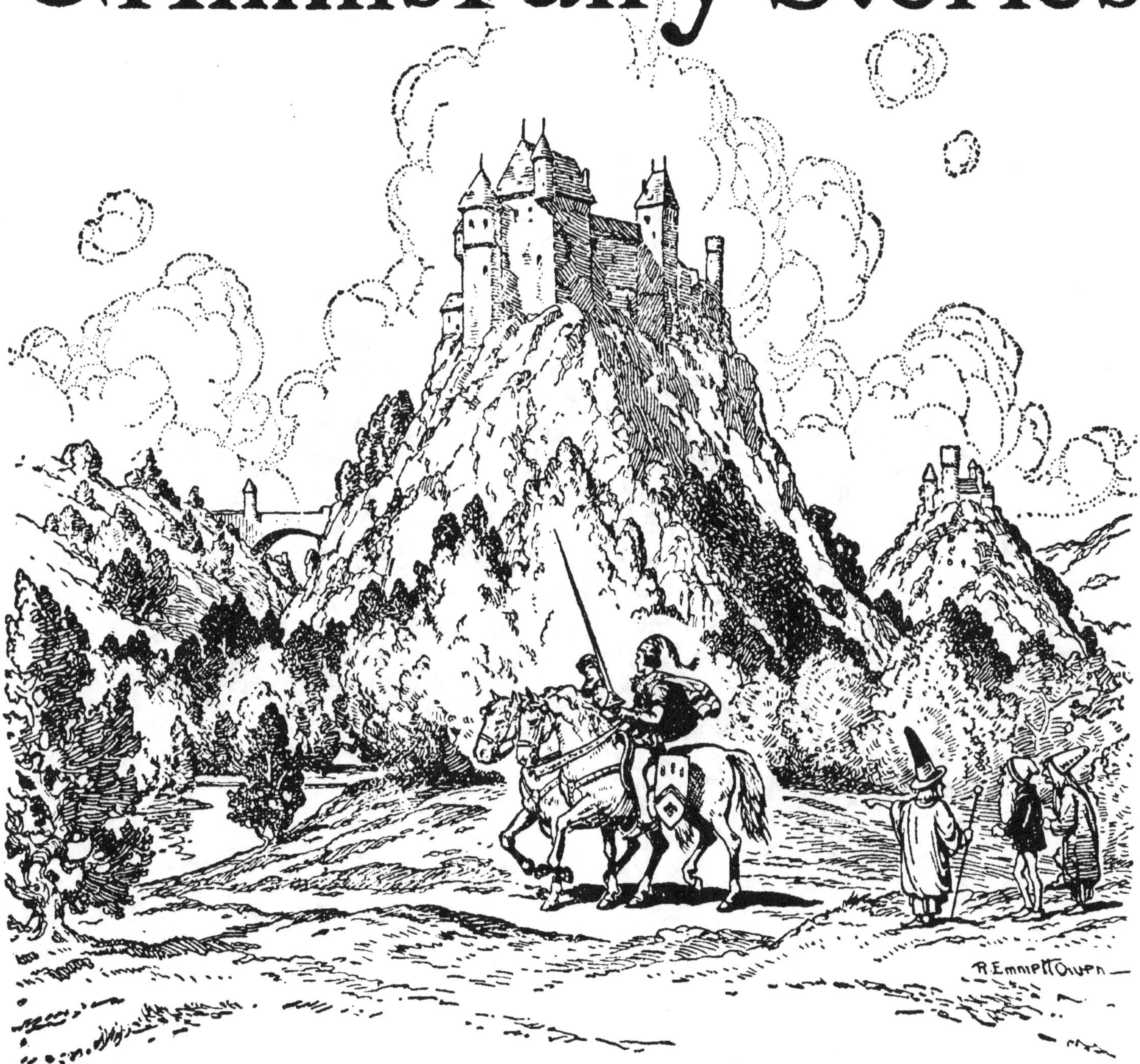

Pen and Ink Sketches by R. Emmett Owen

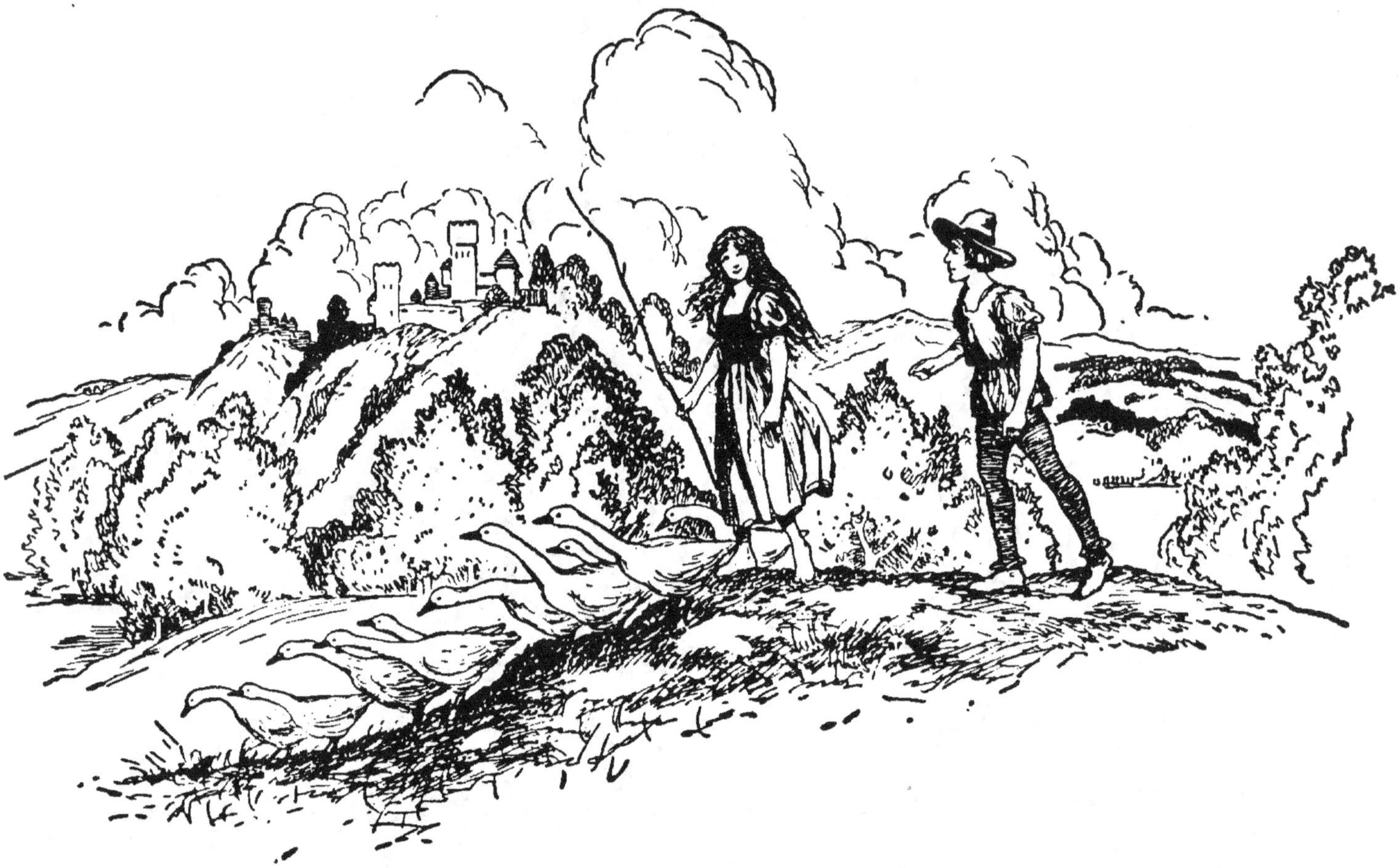

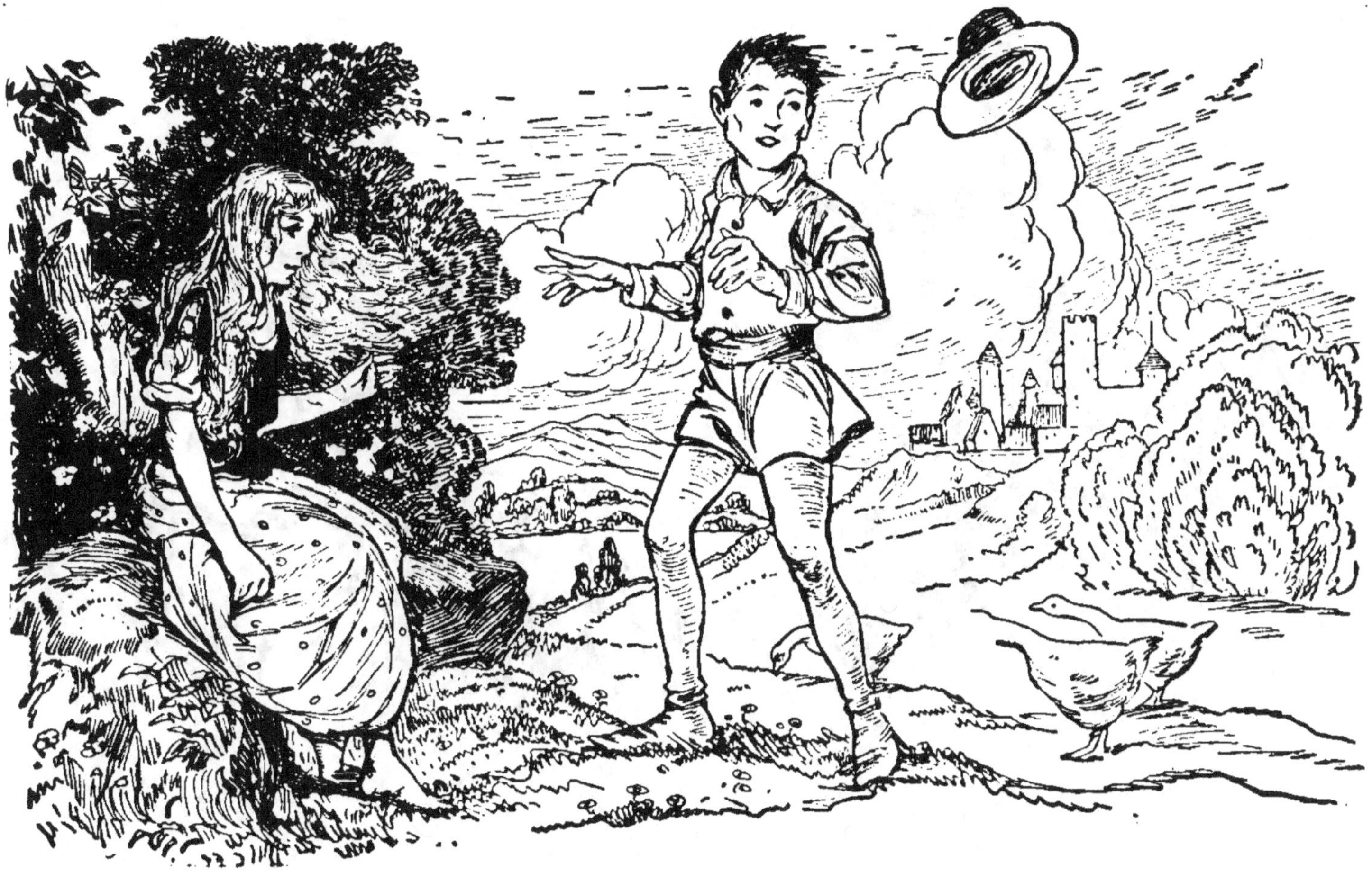

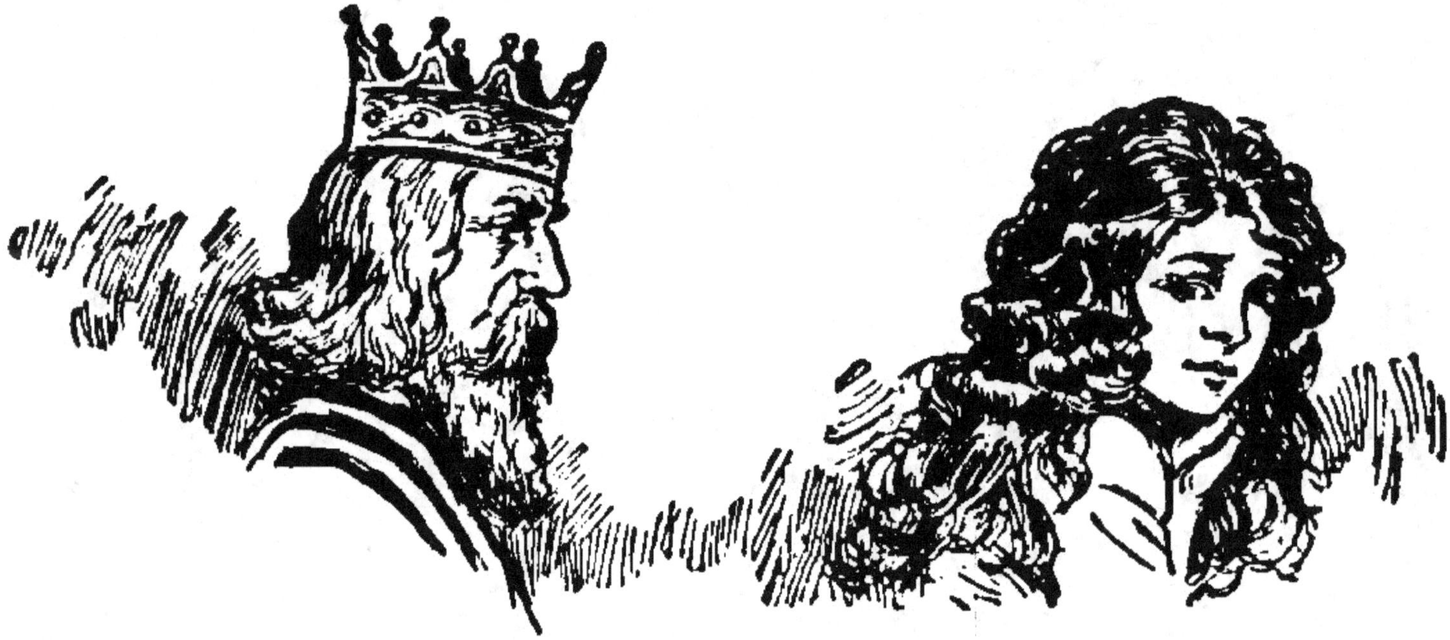

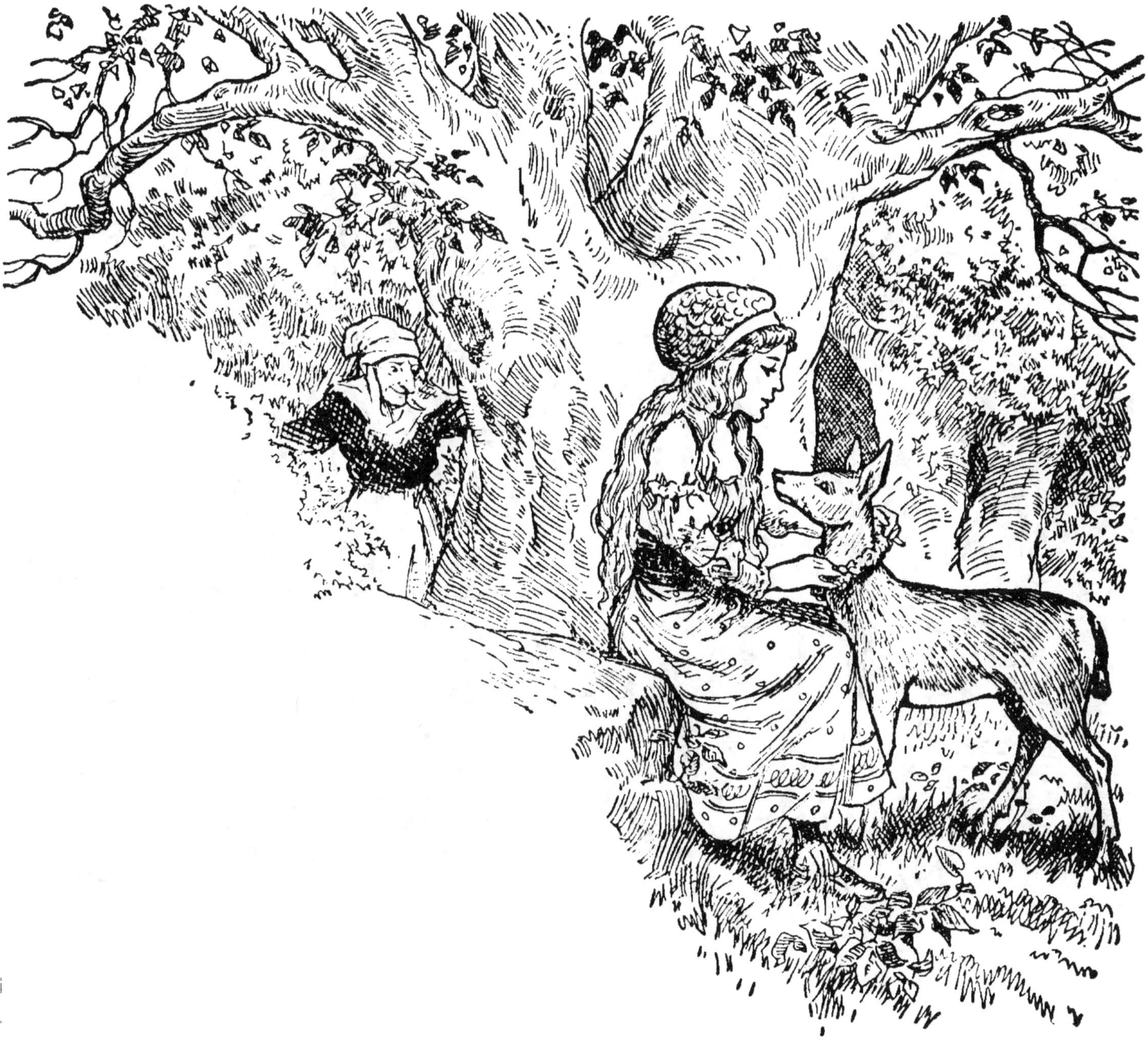

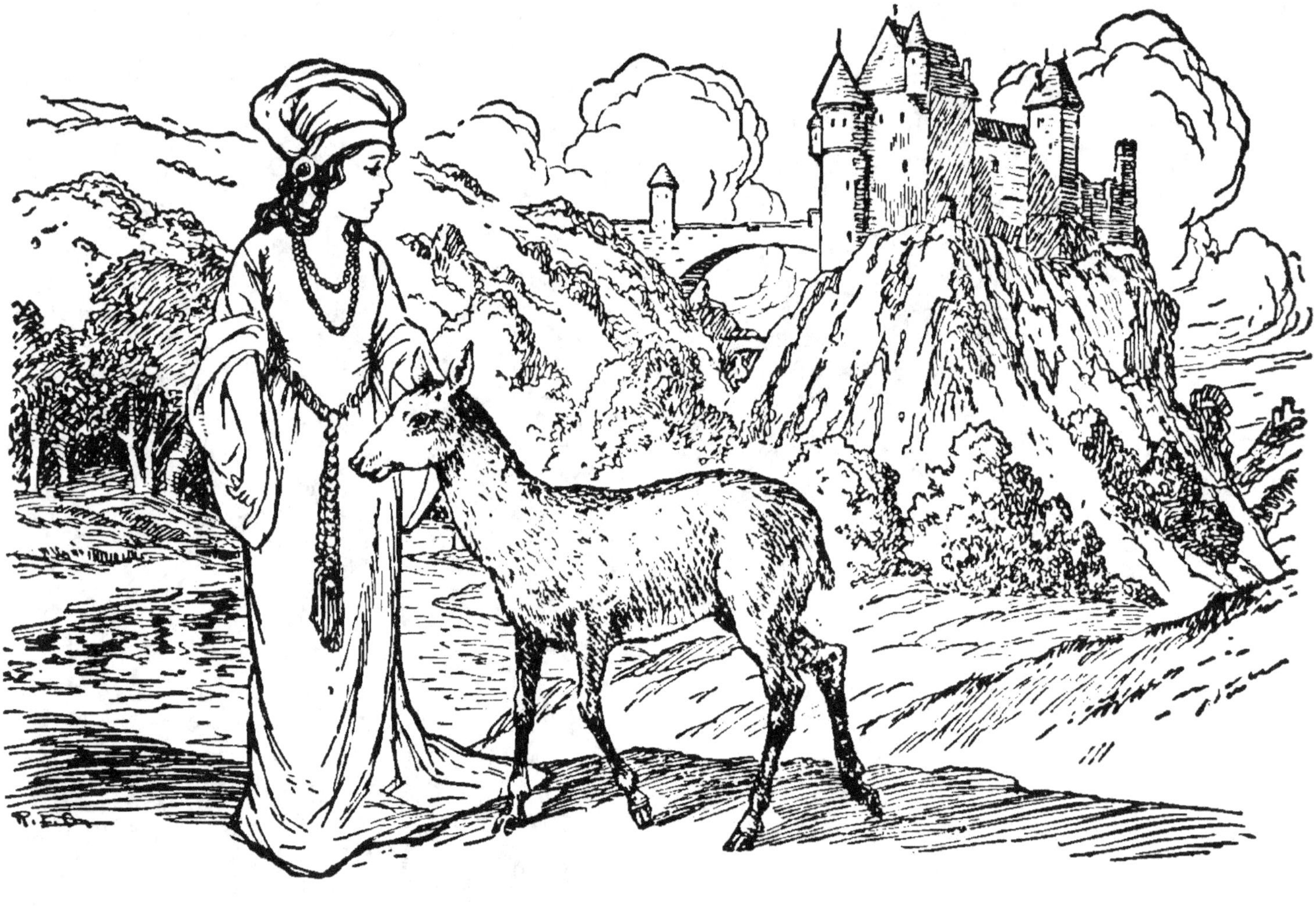

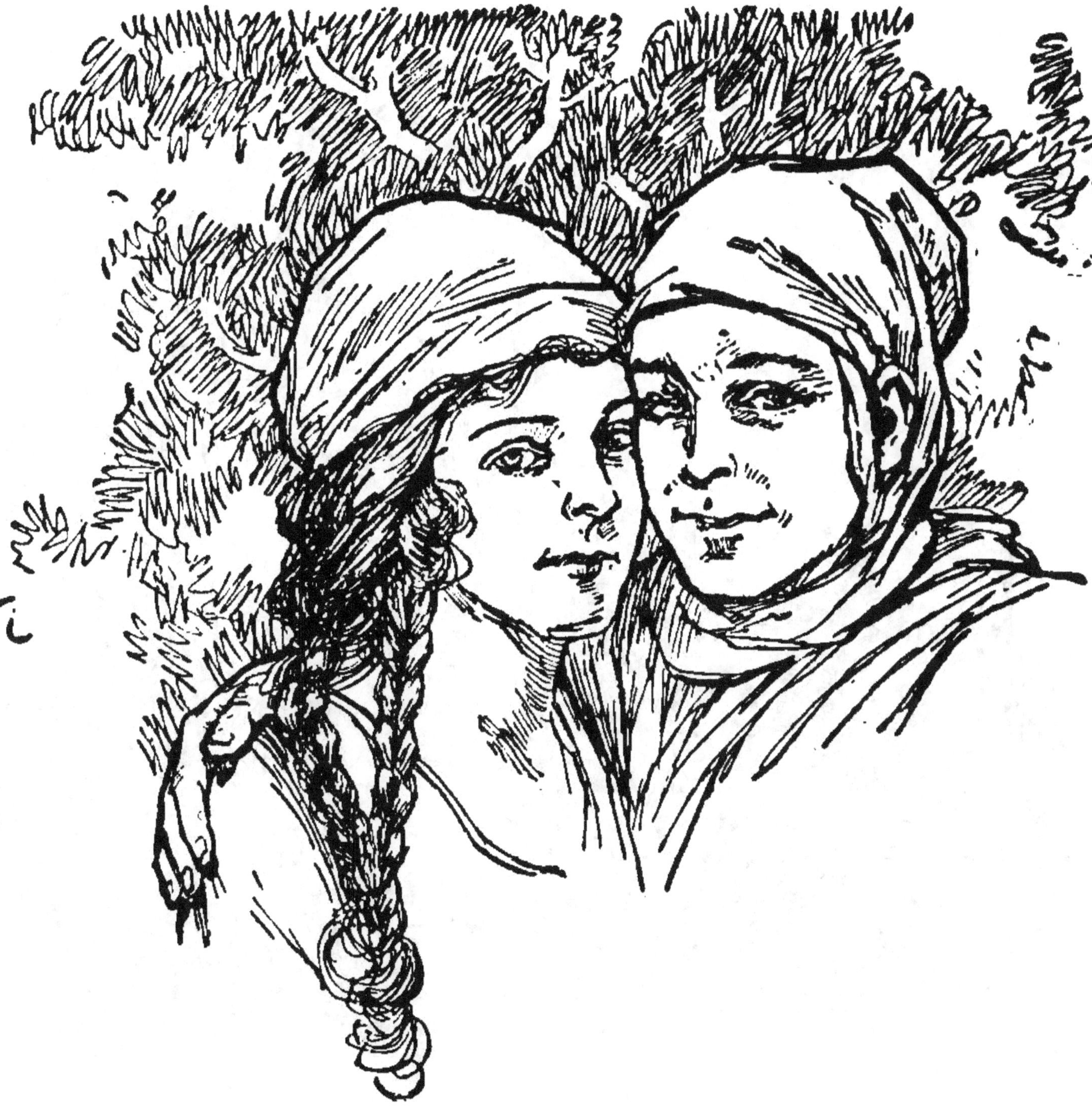

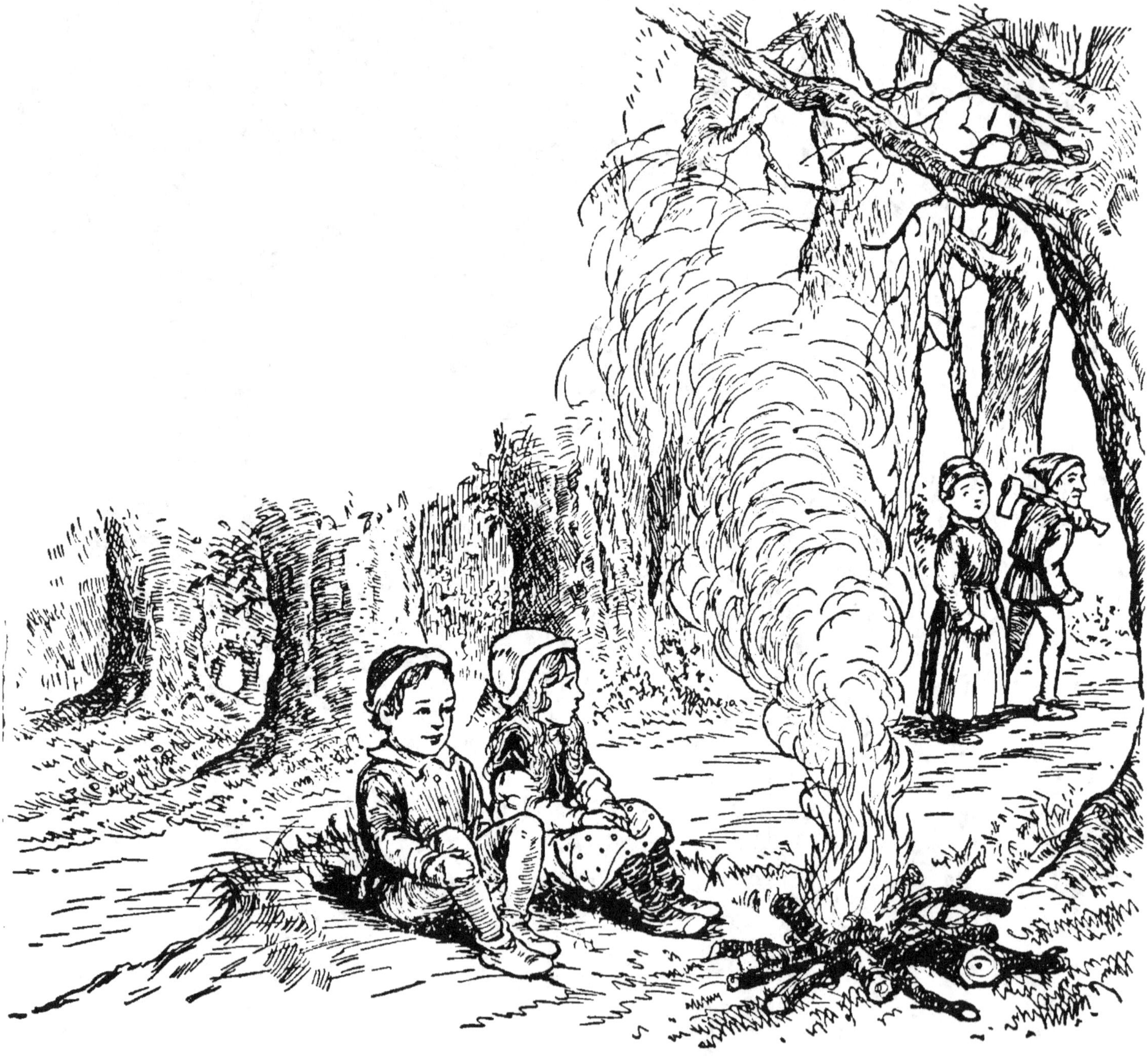

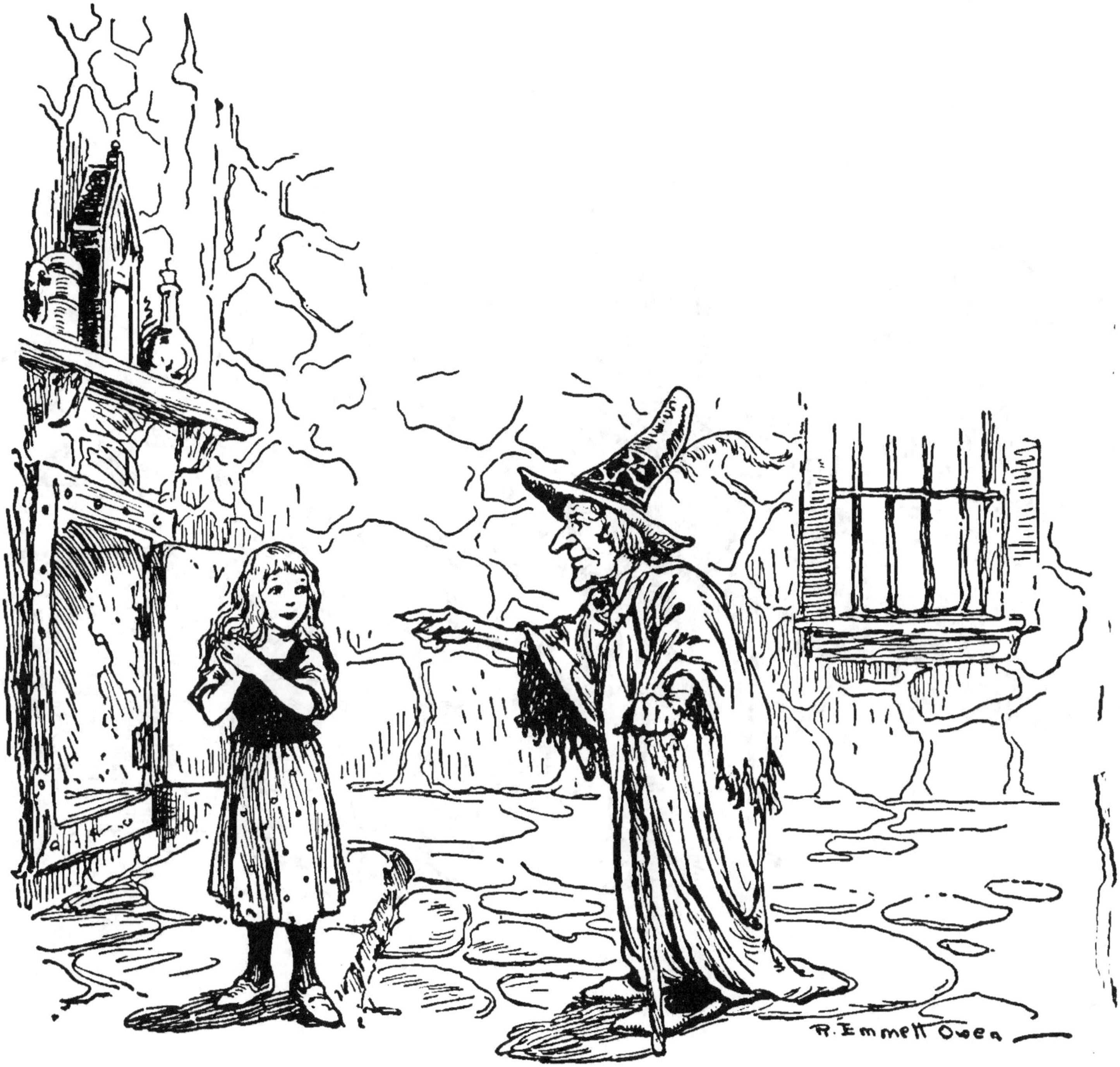
R. Emmett Owen

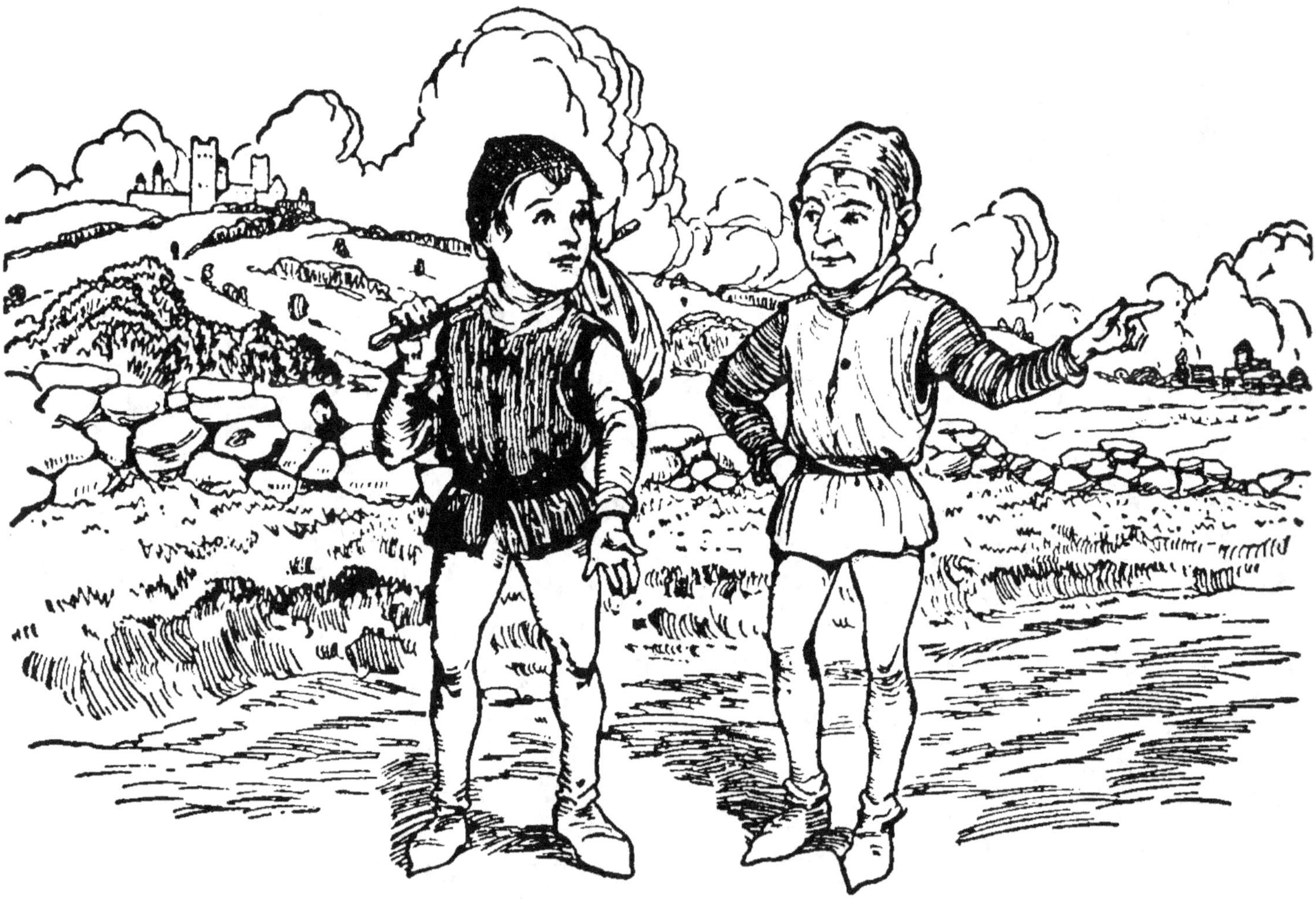

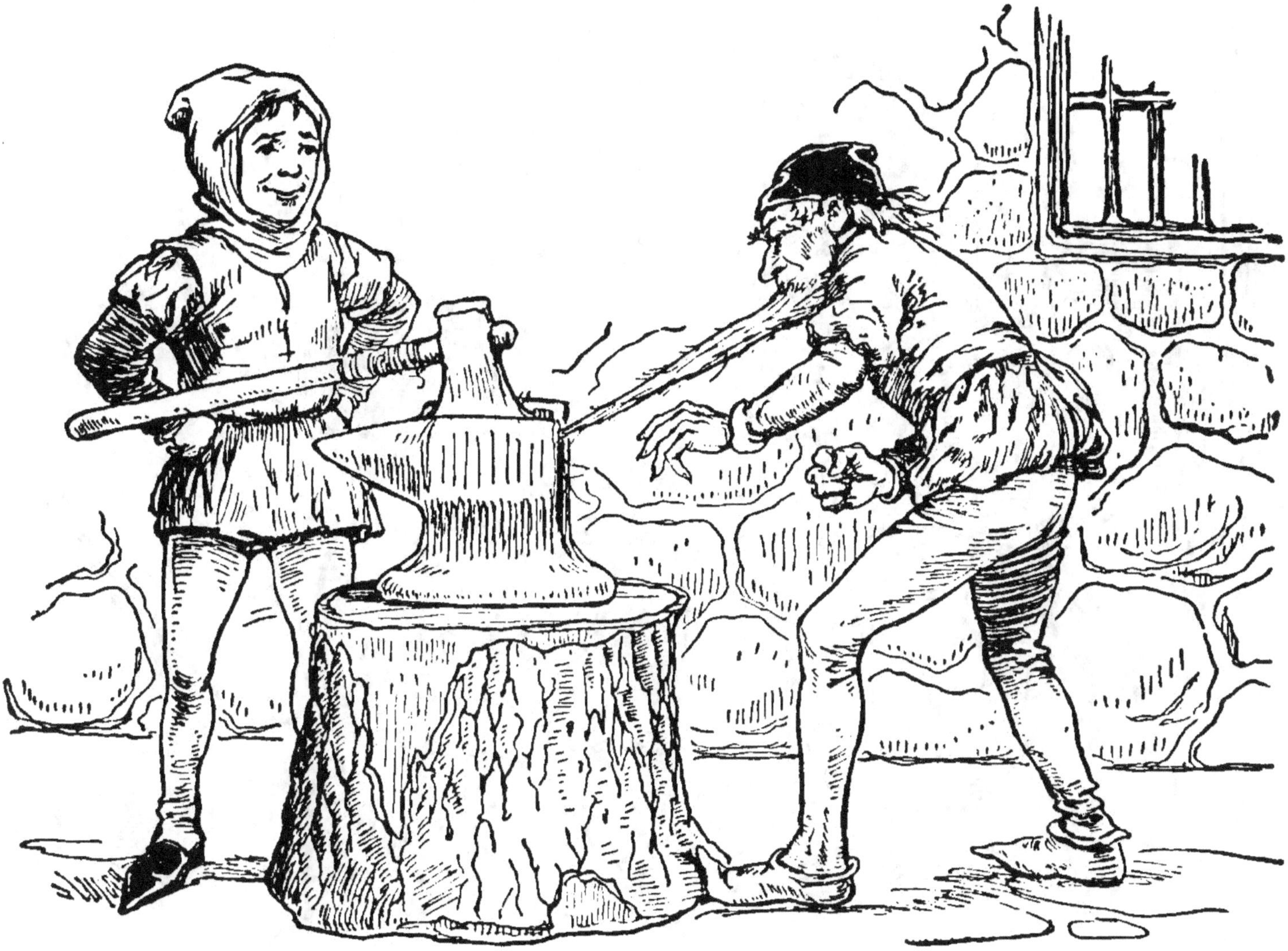

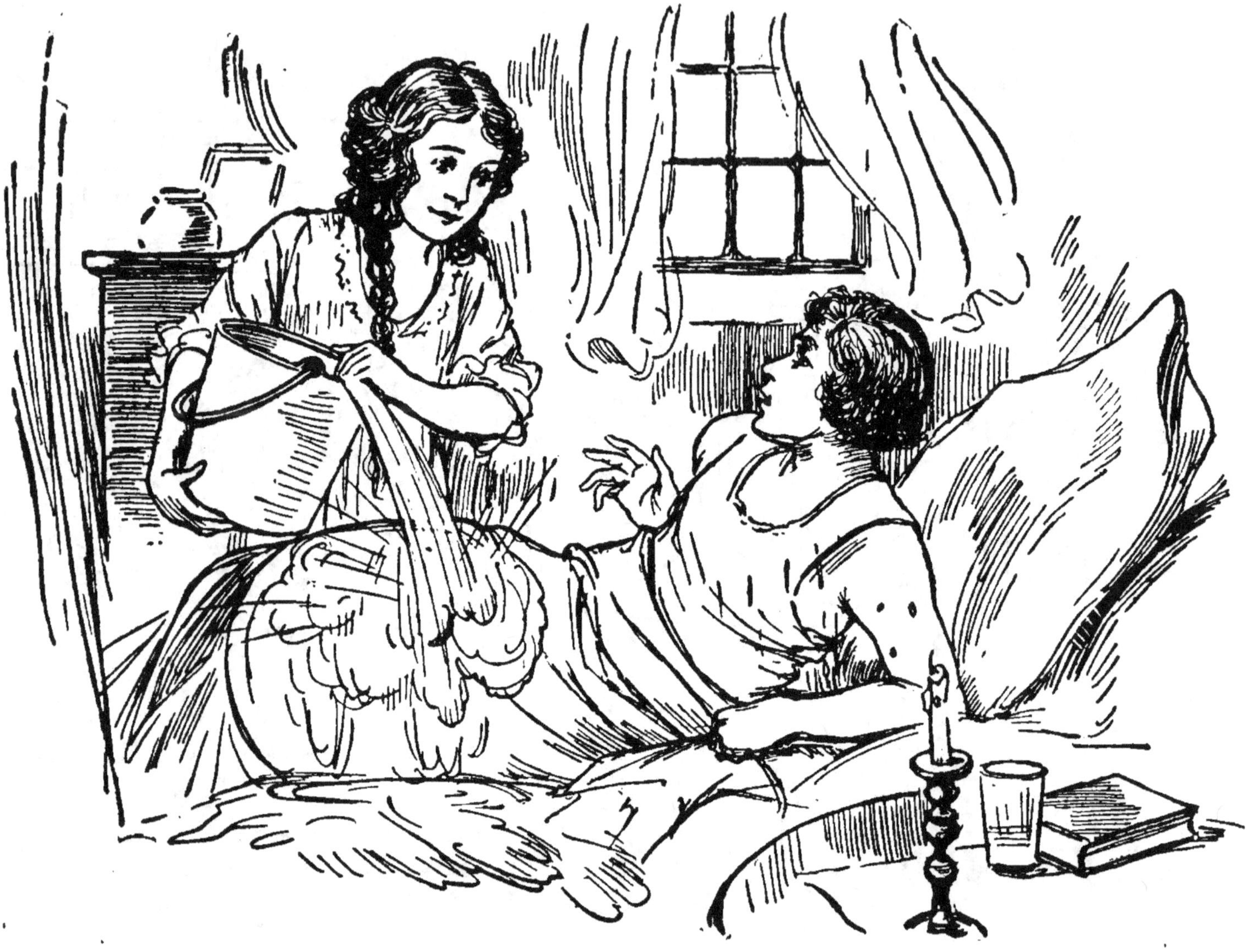

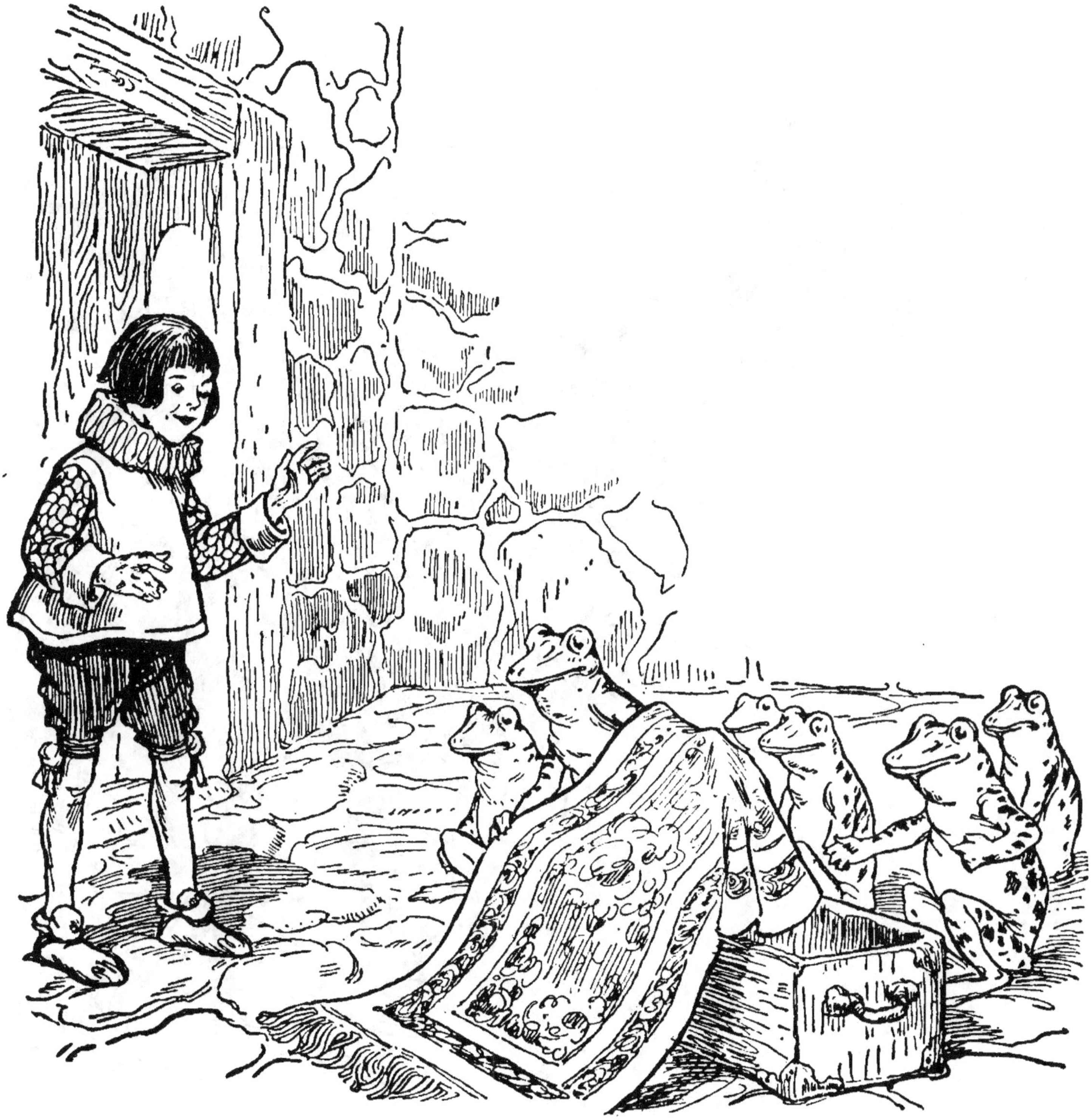

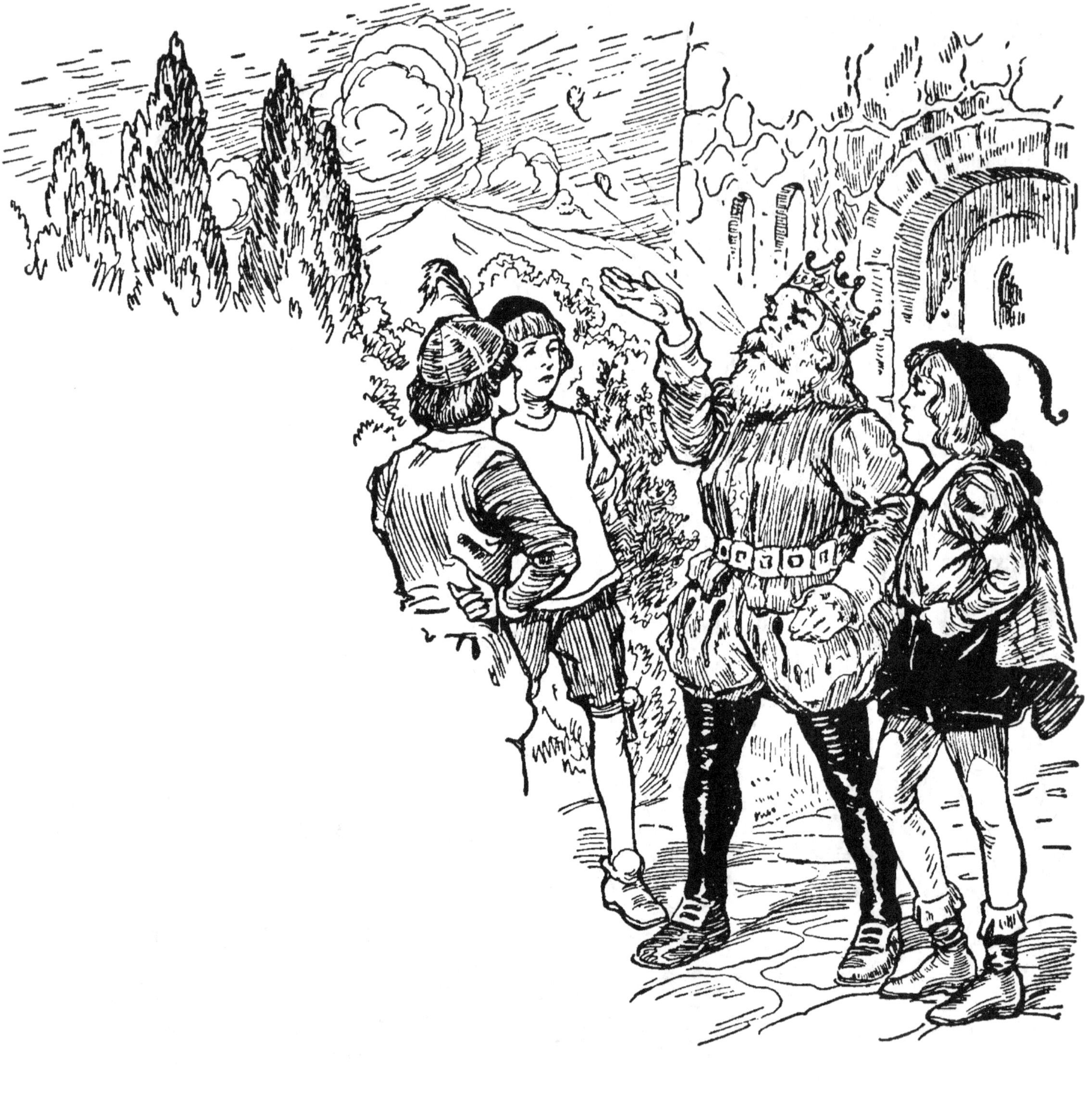

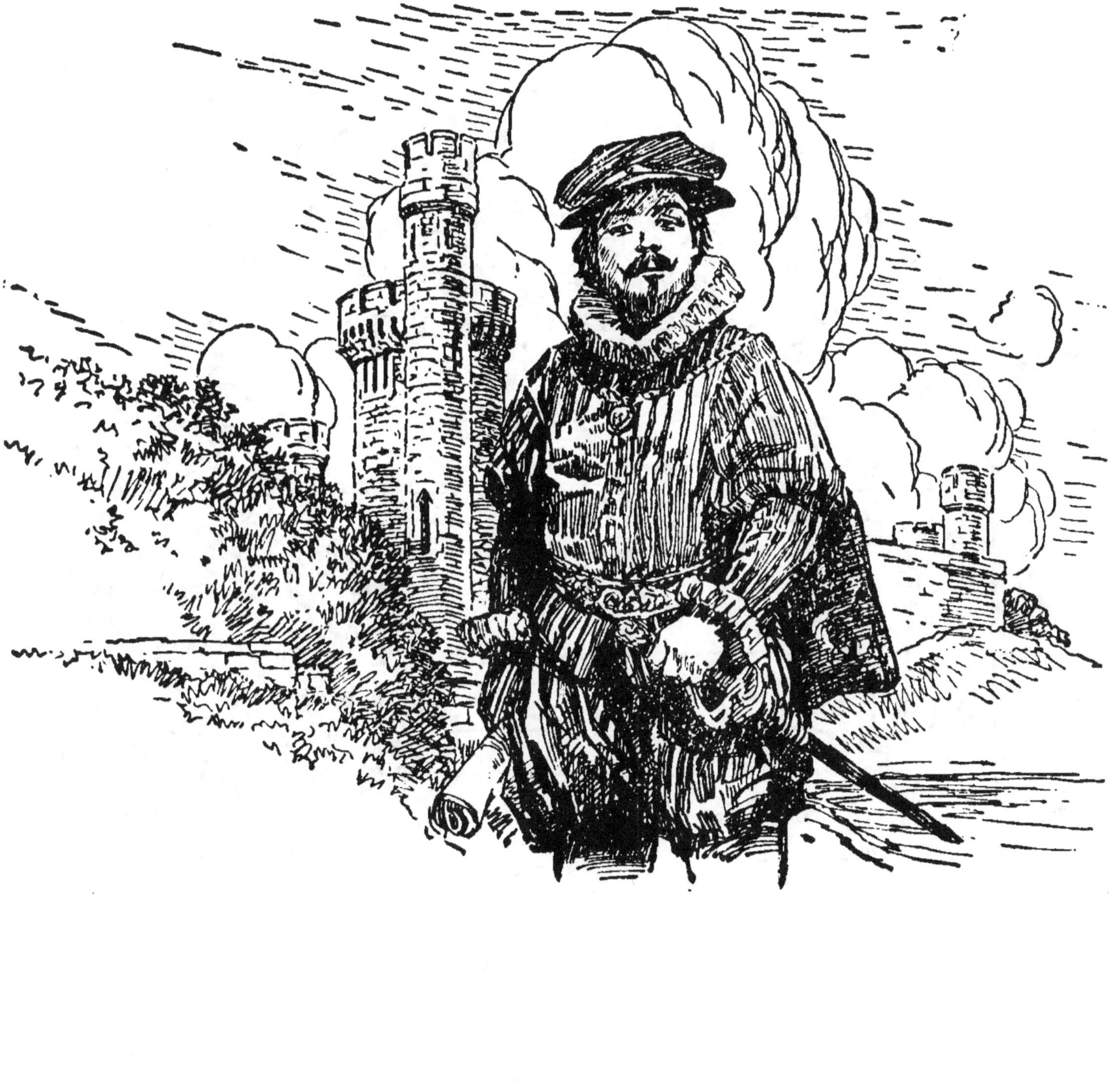

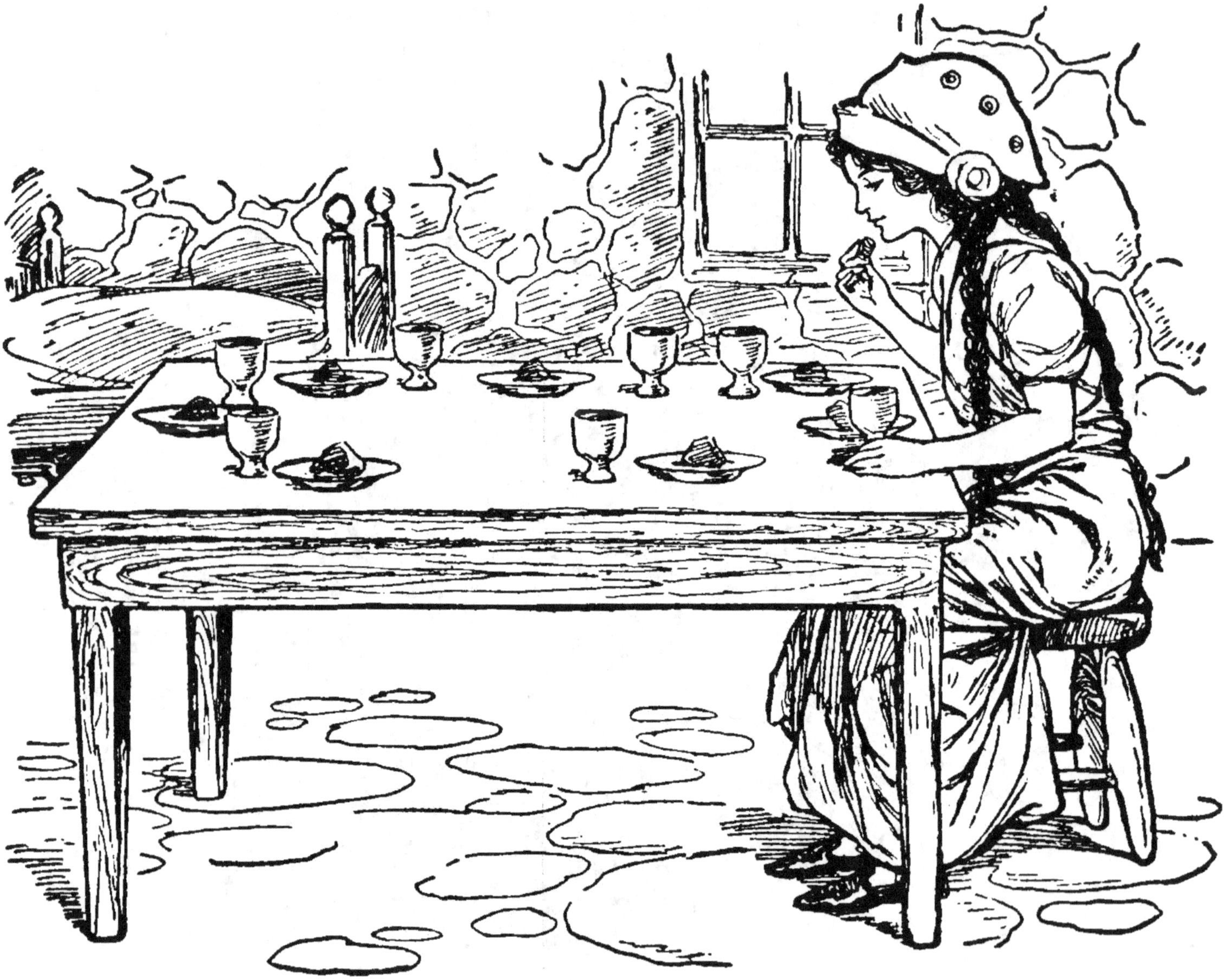

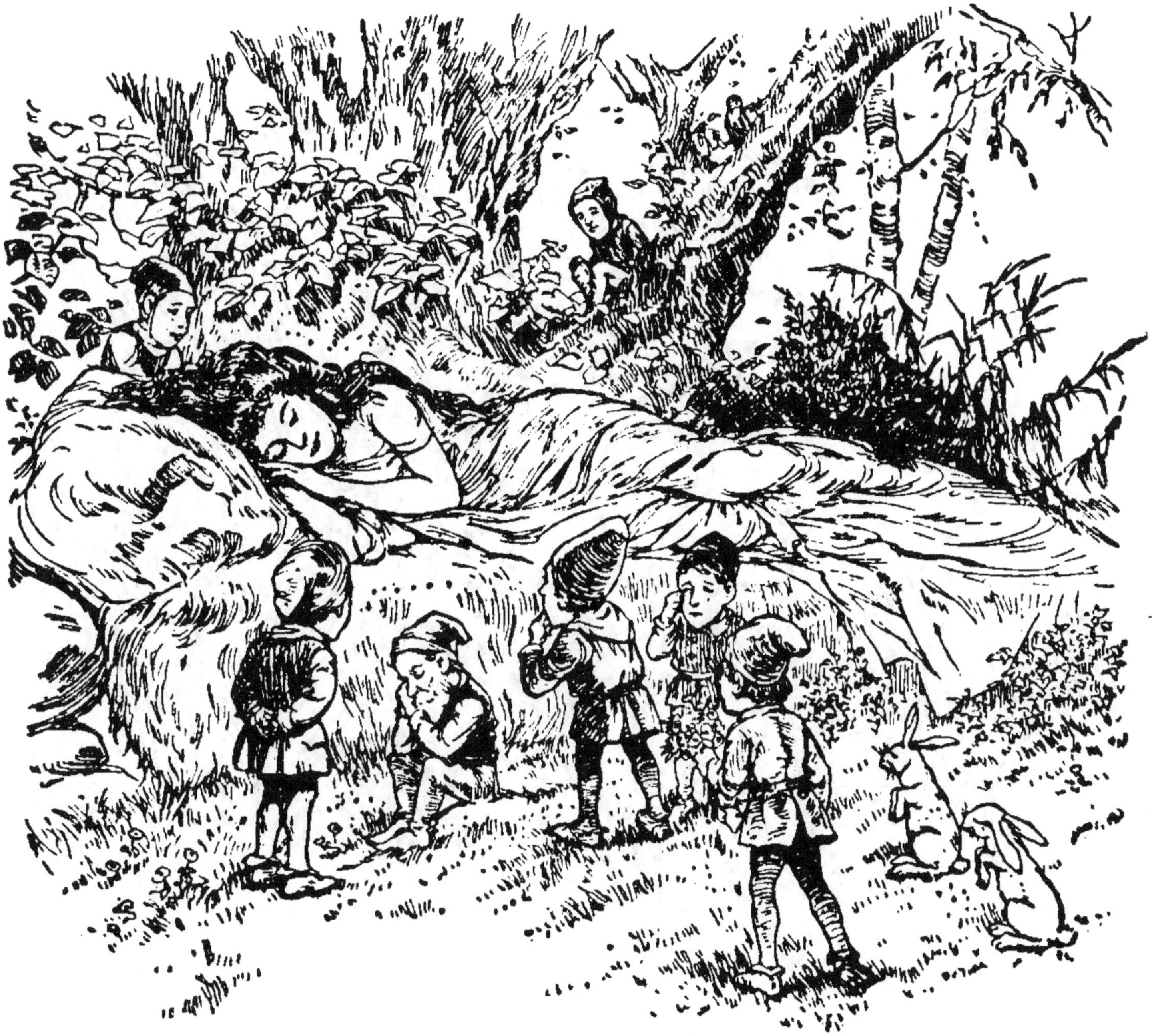

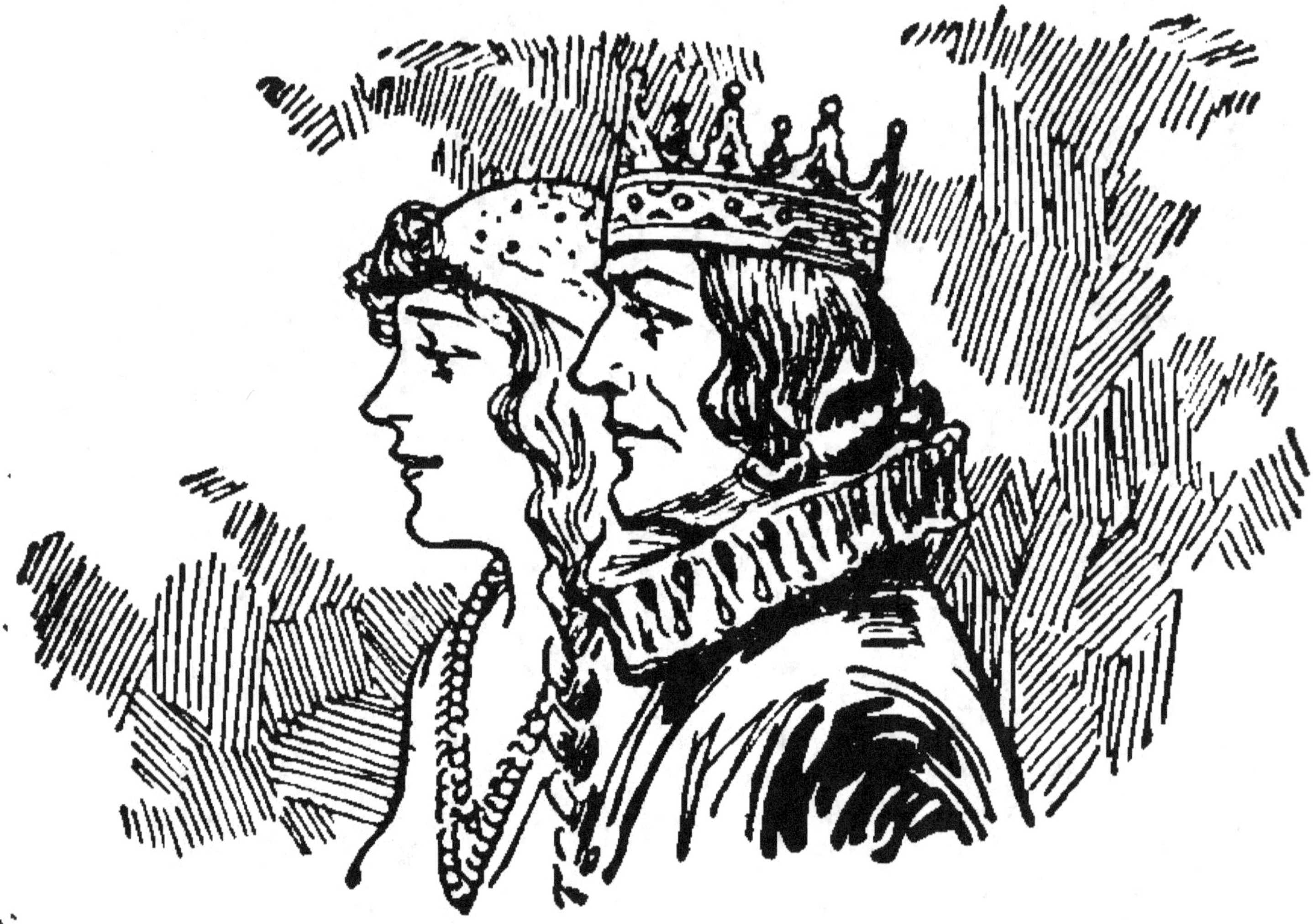

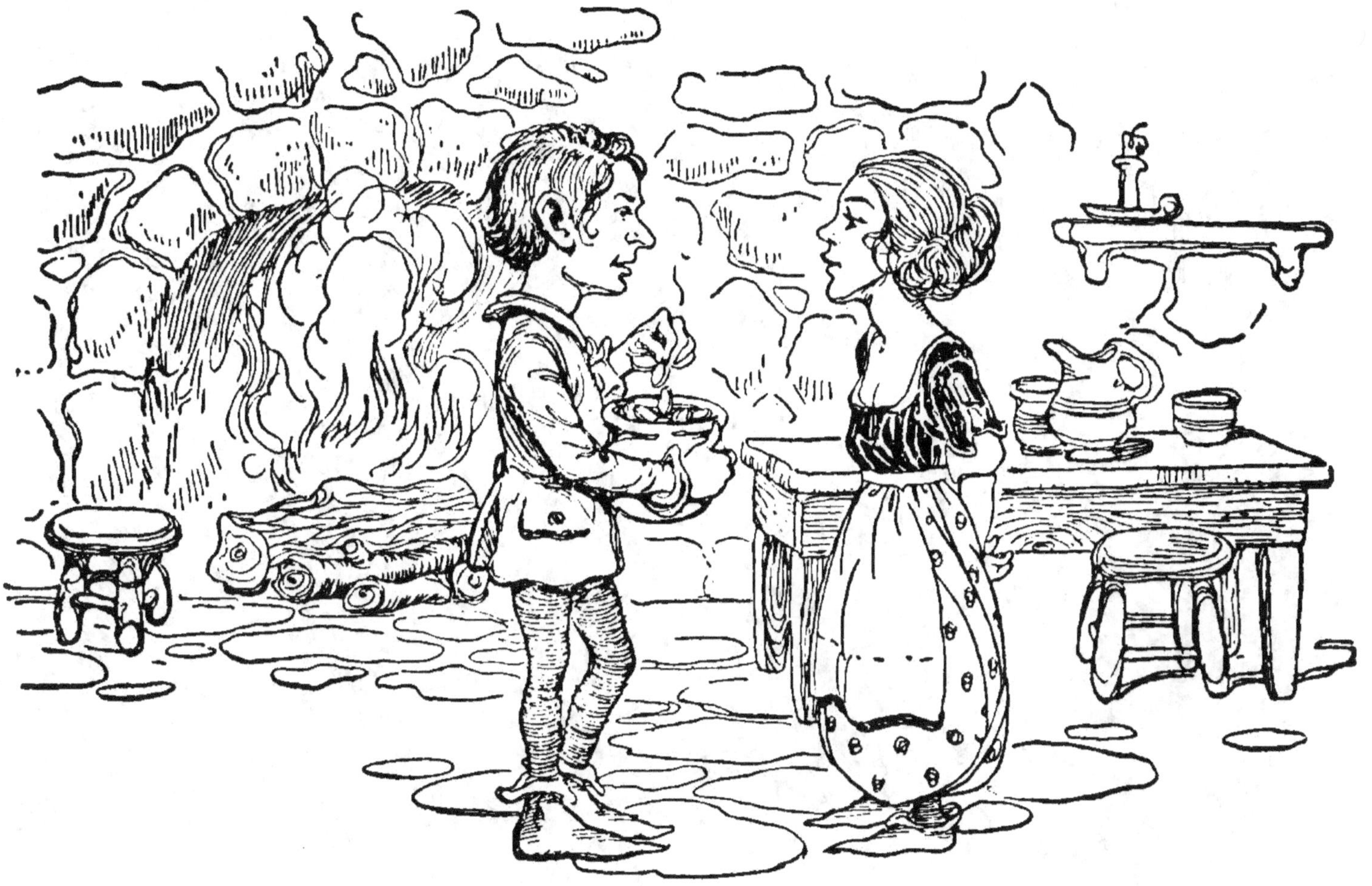

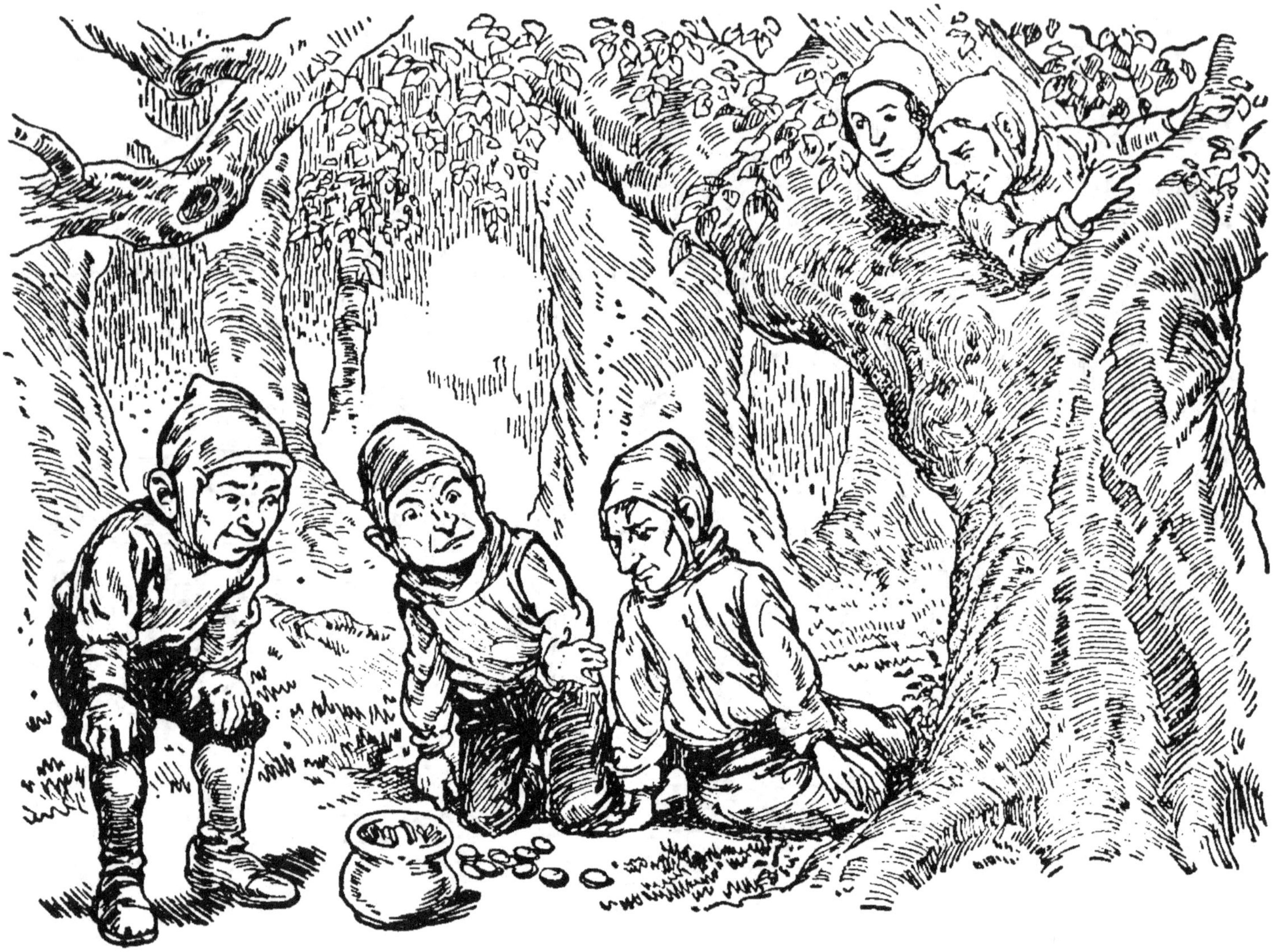

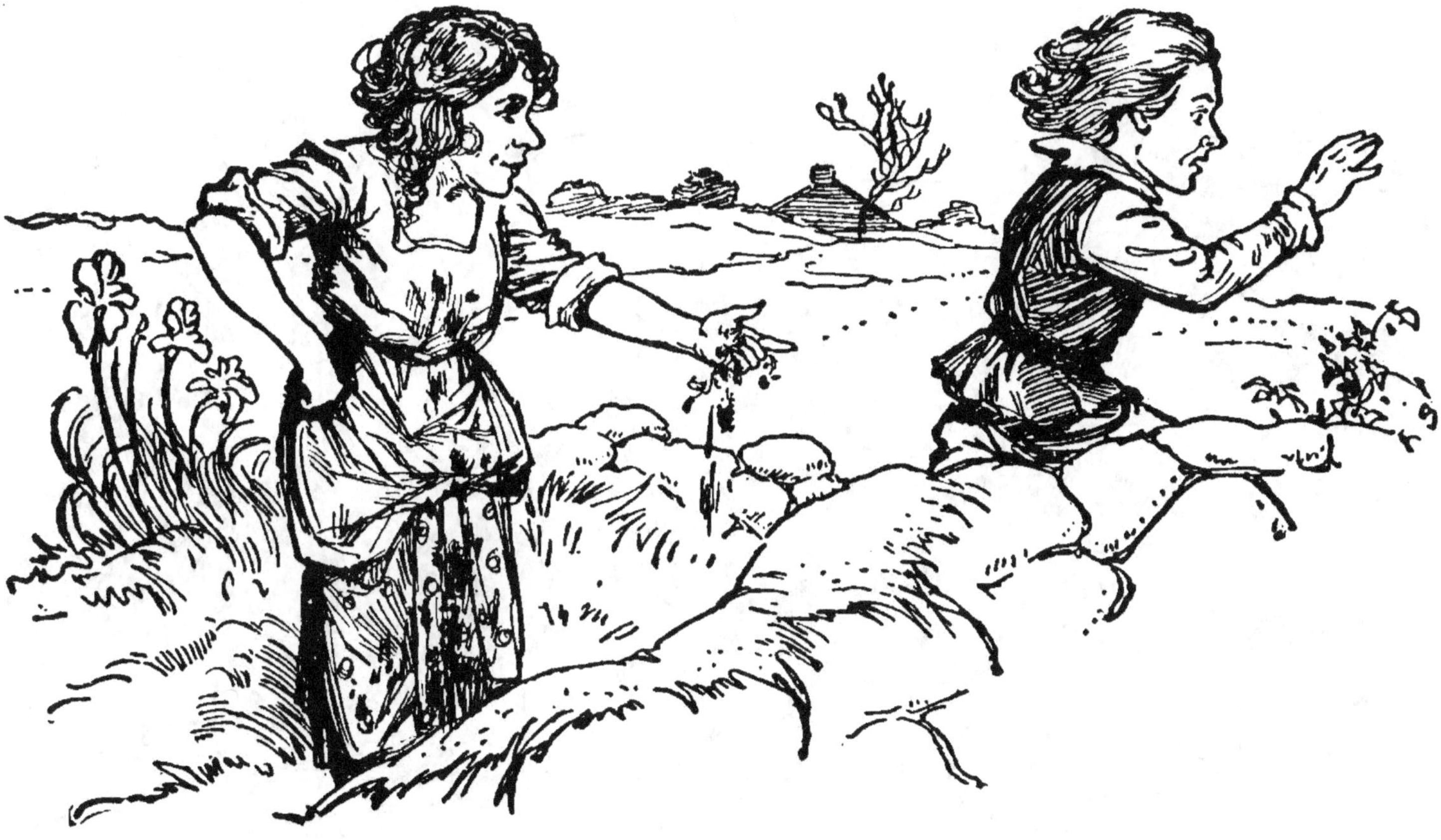

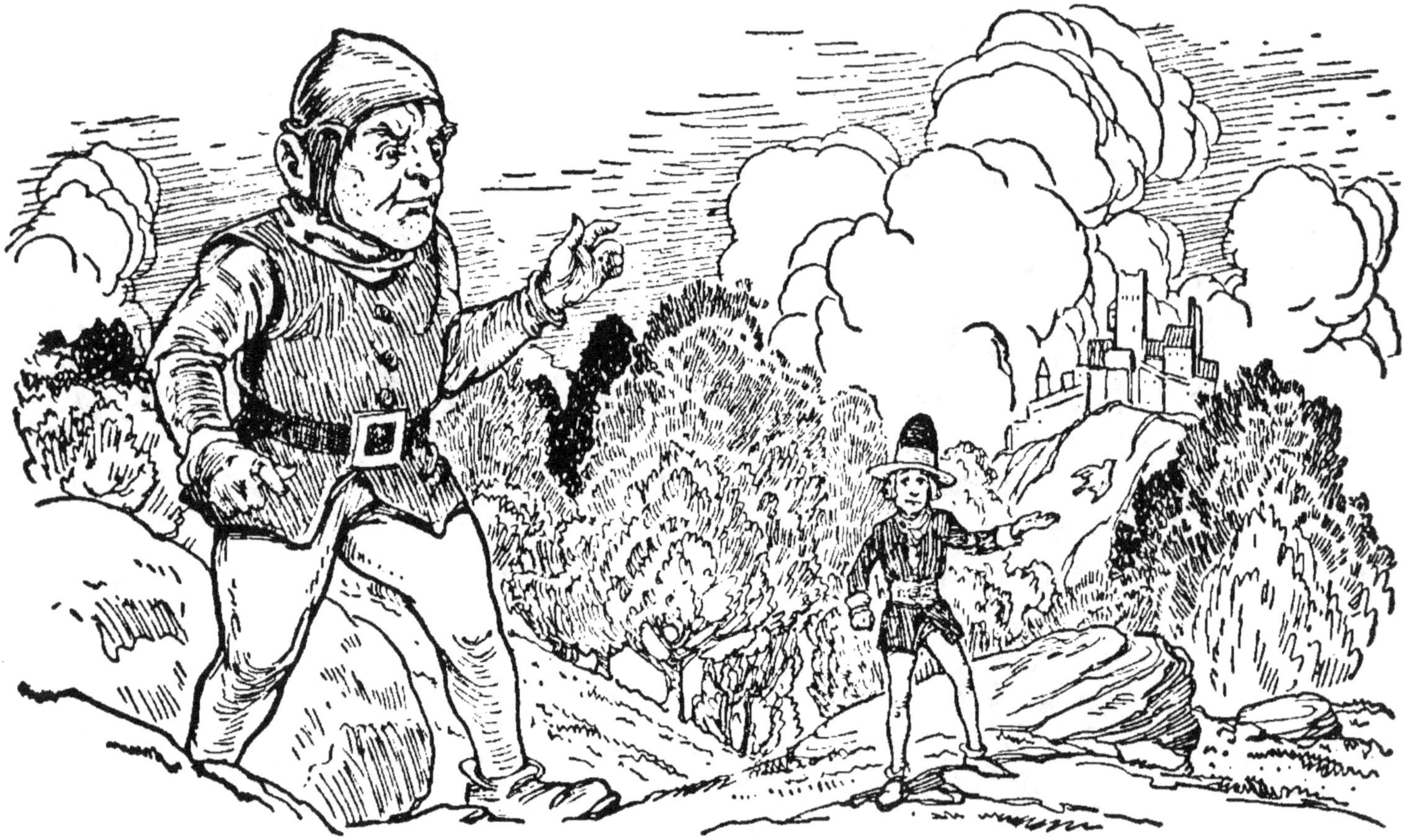

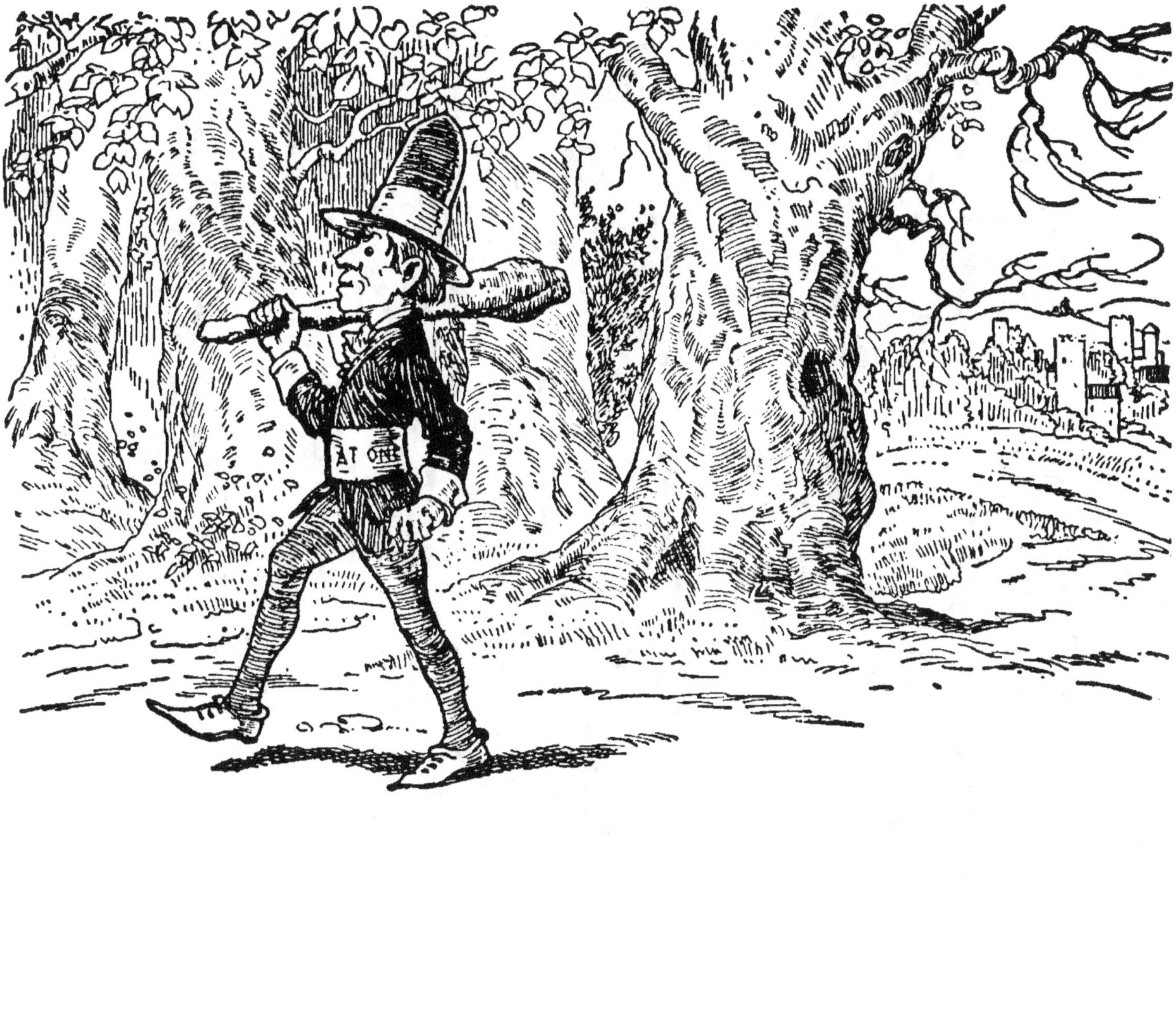
AT ONE

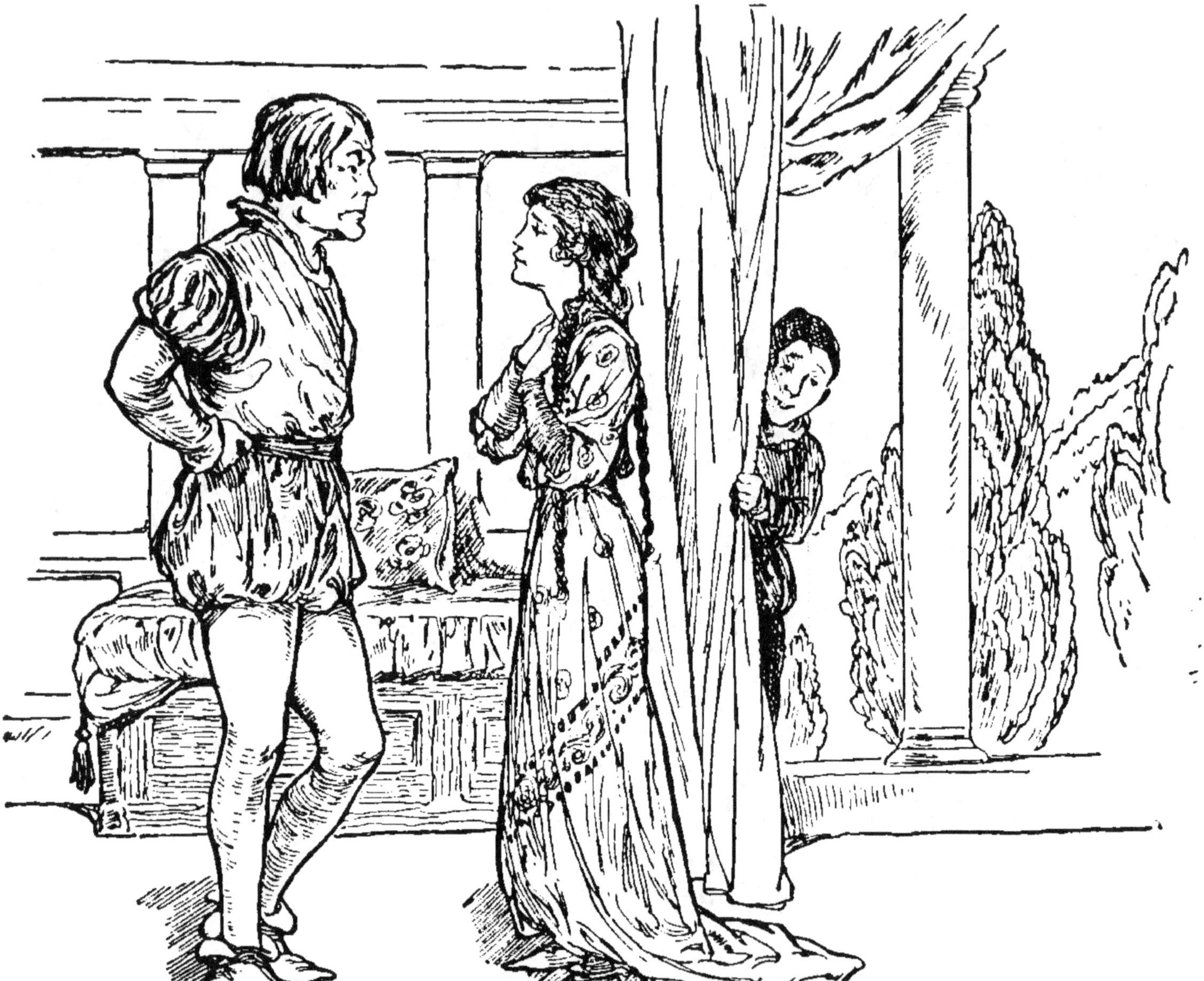

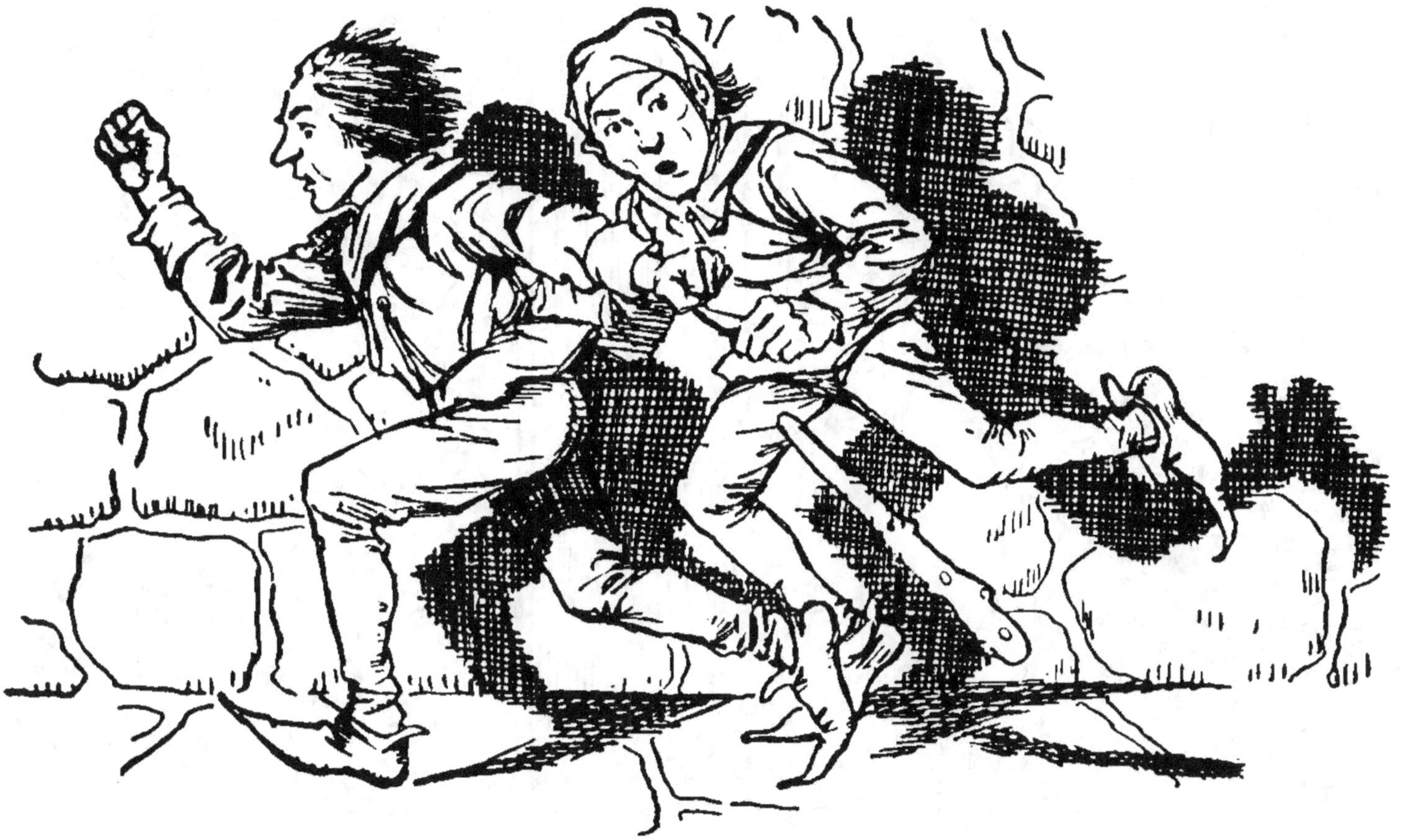

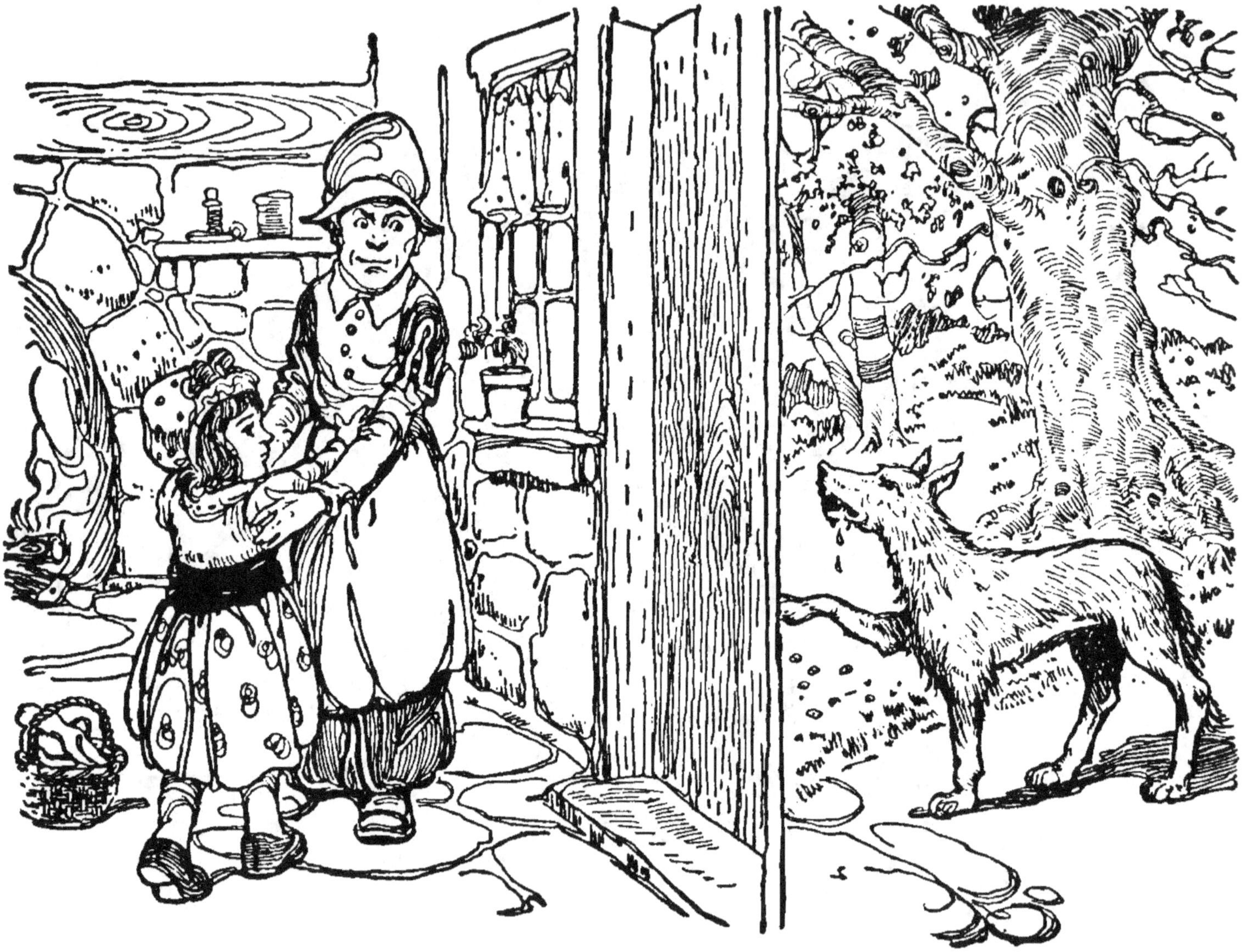

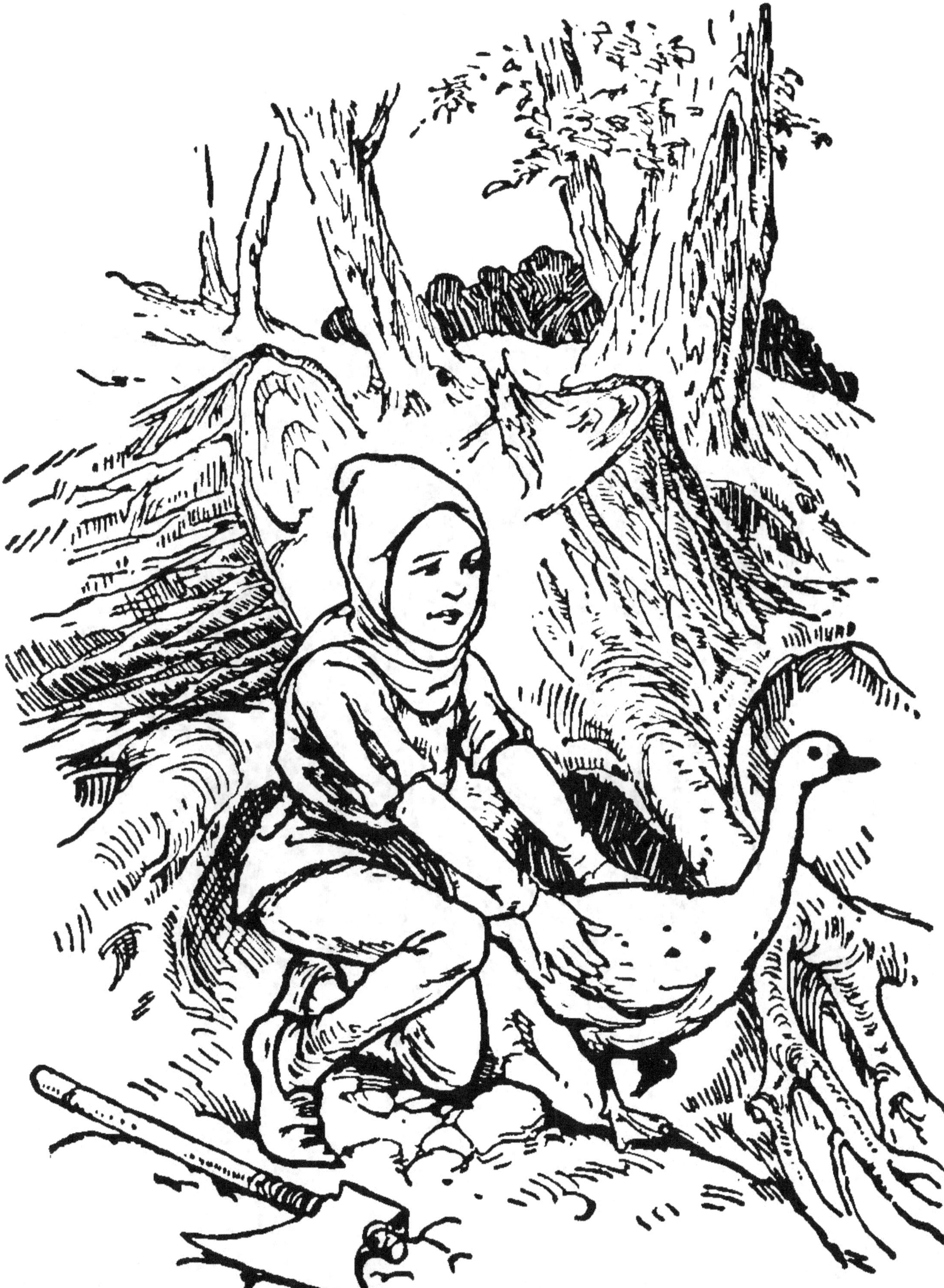

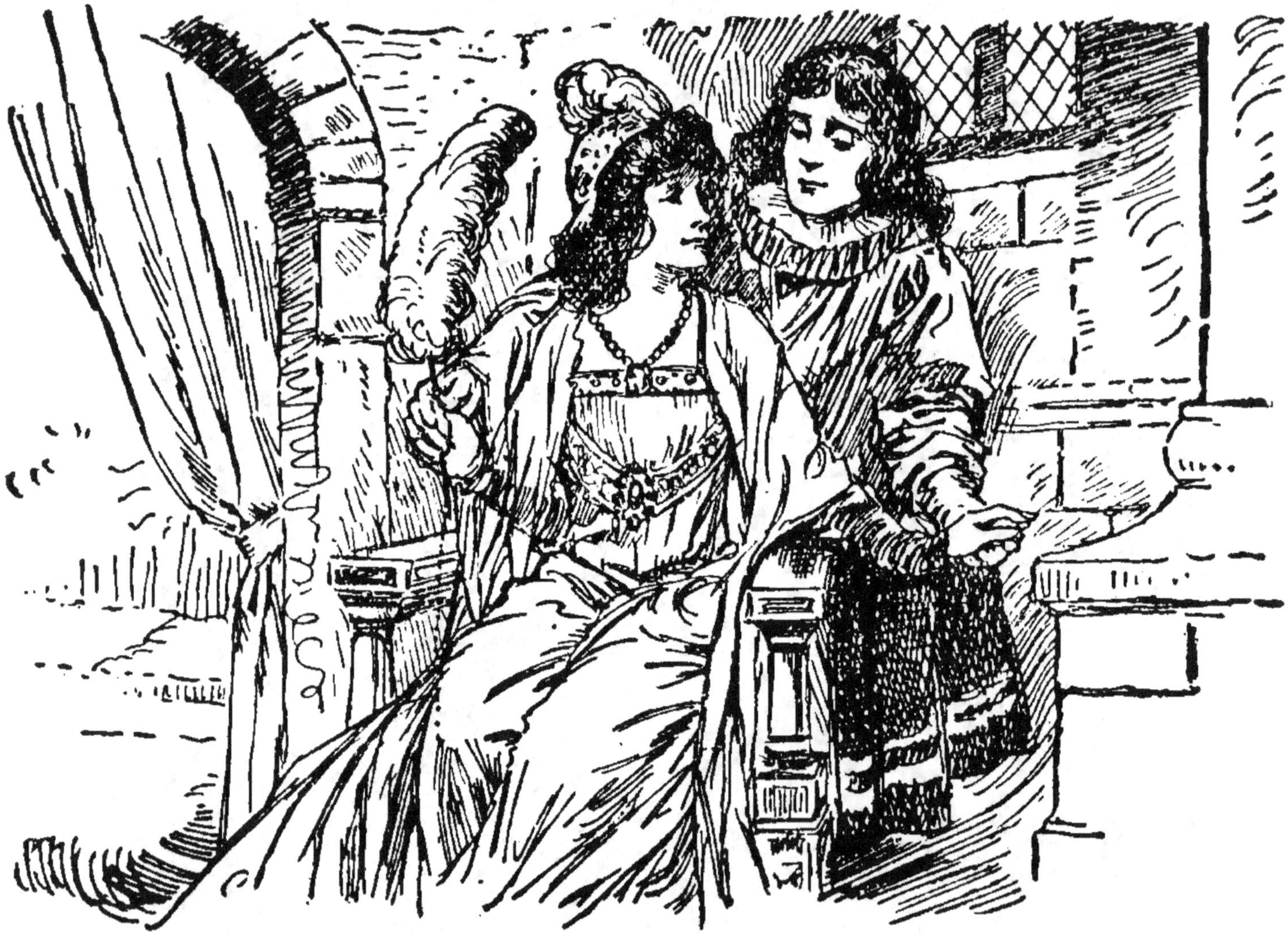

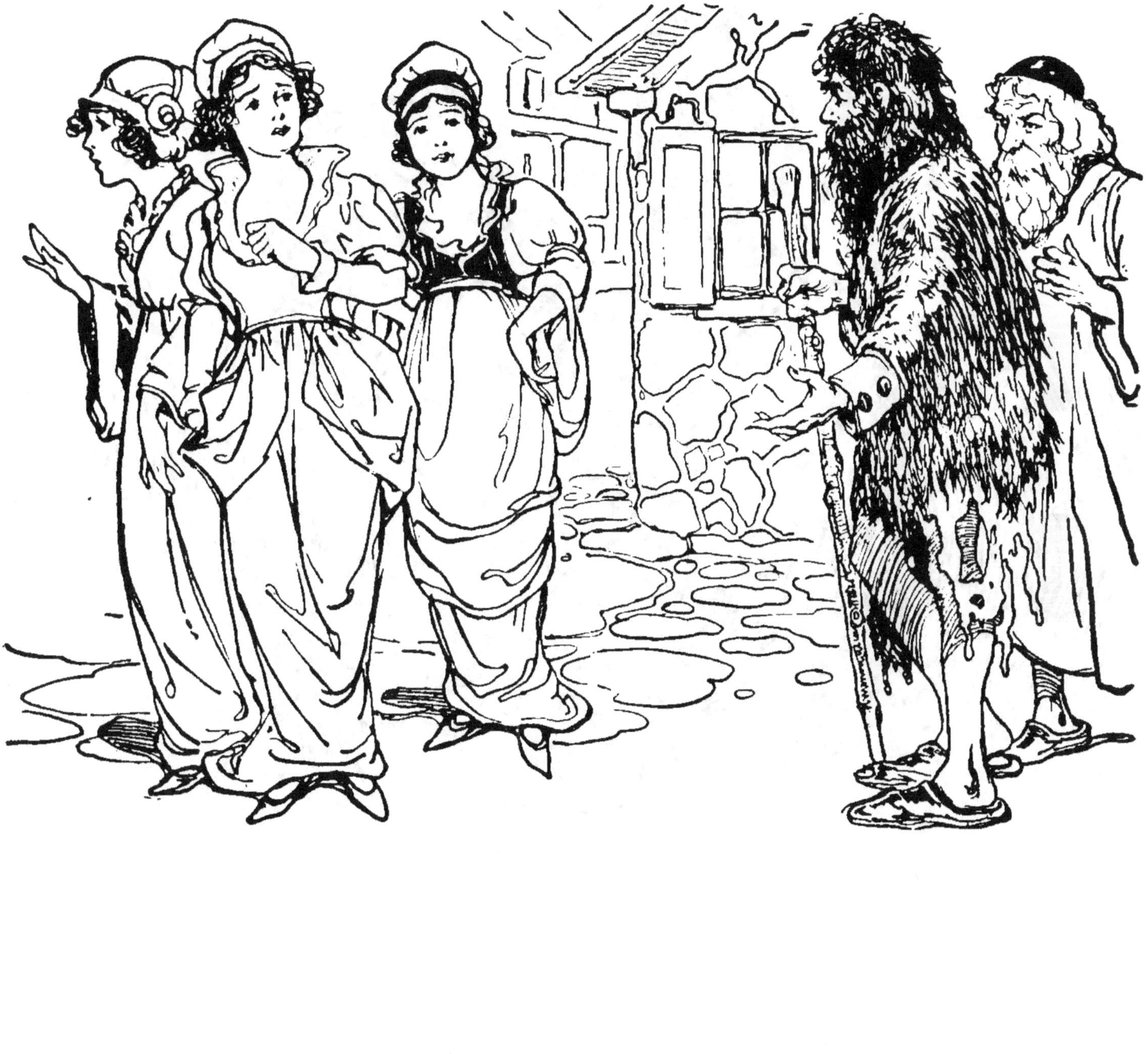

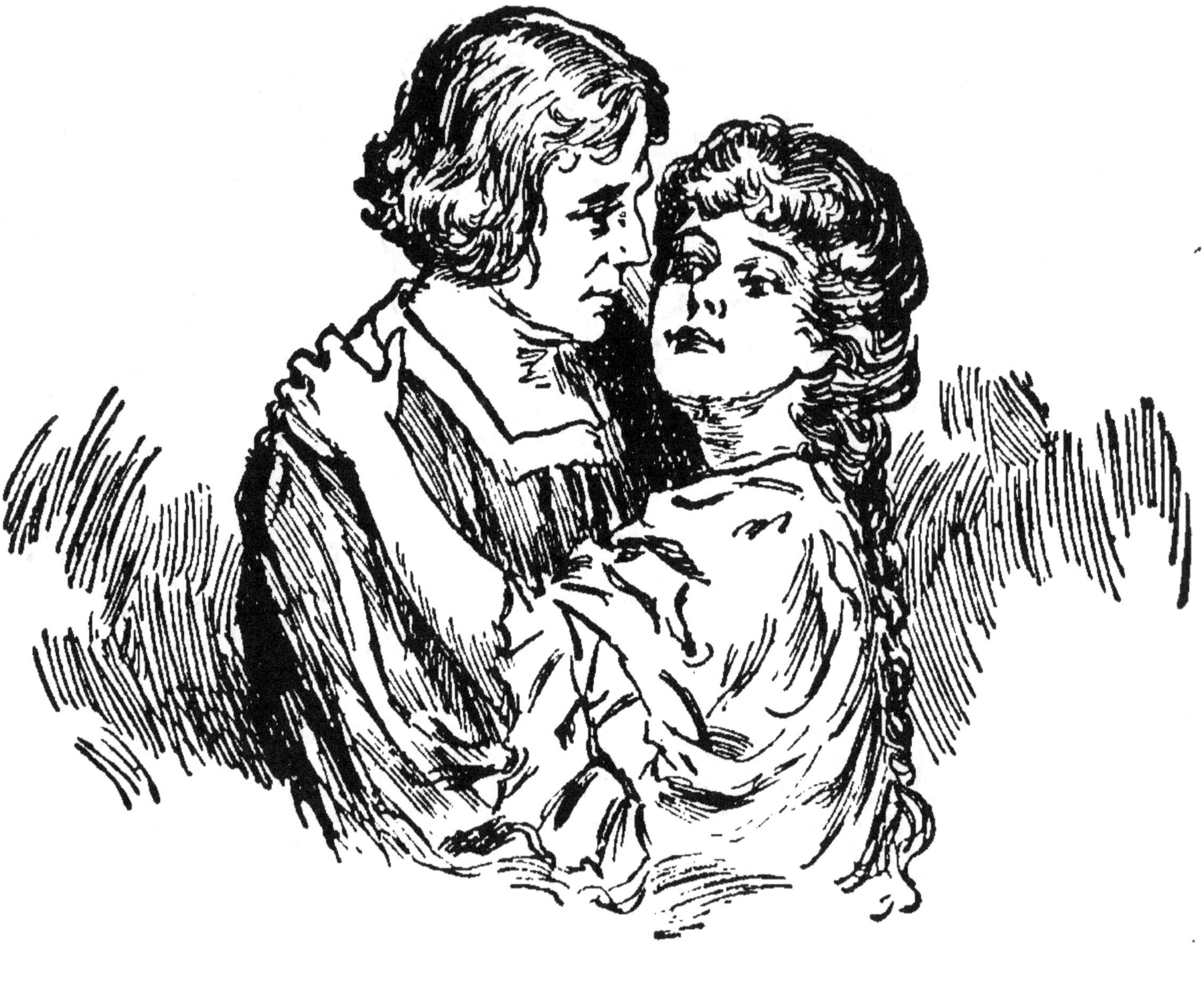

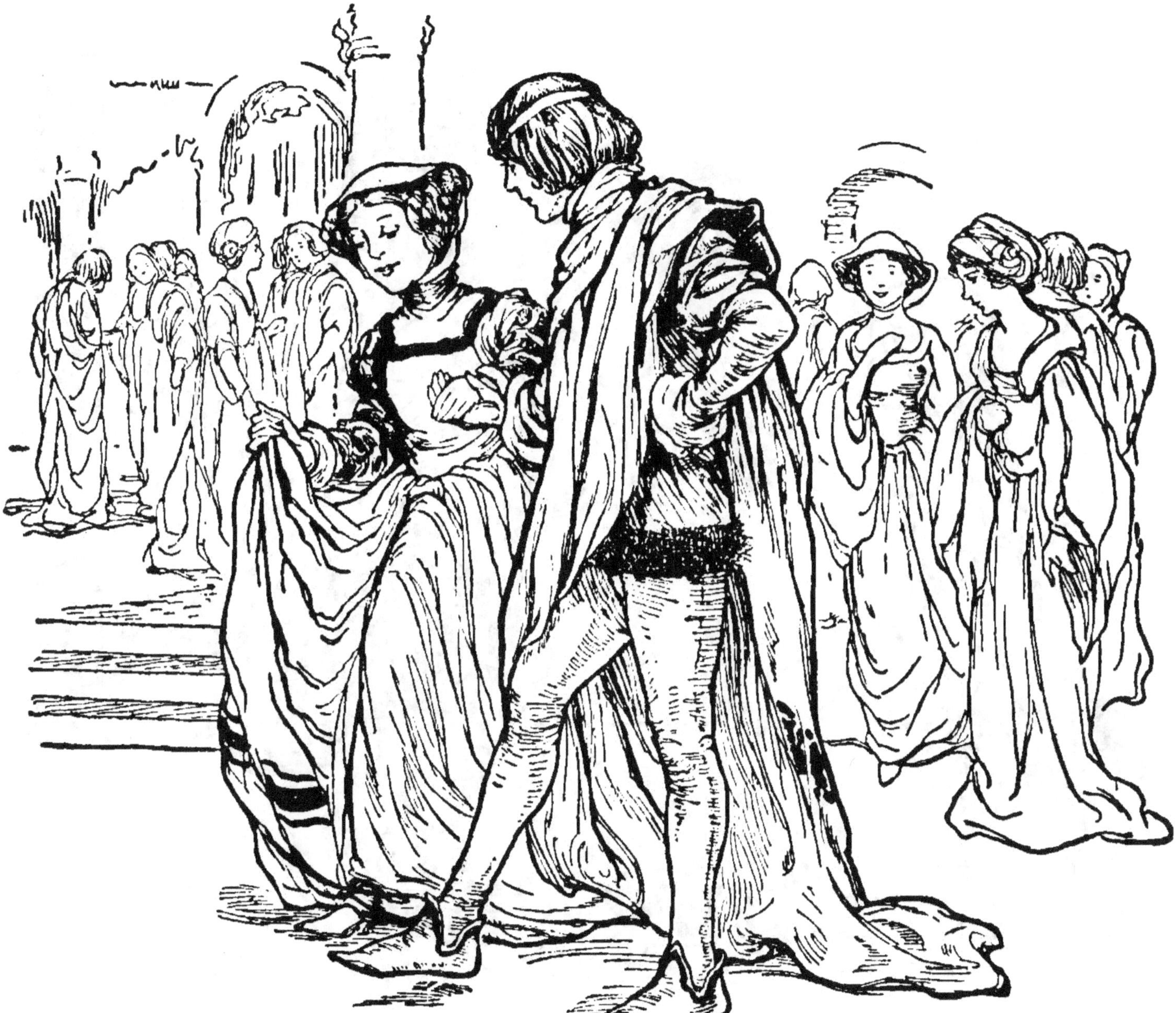

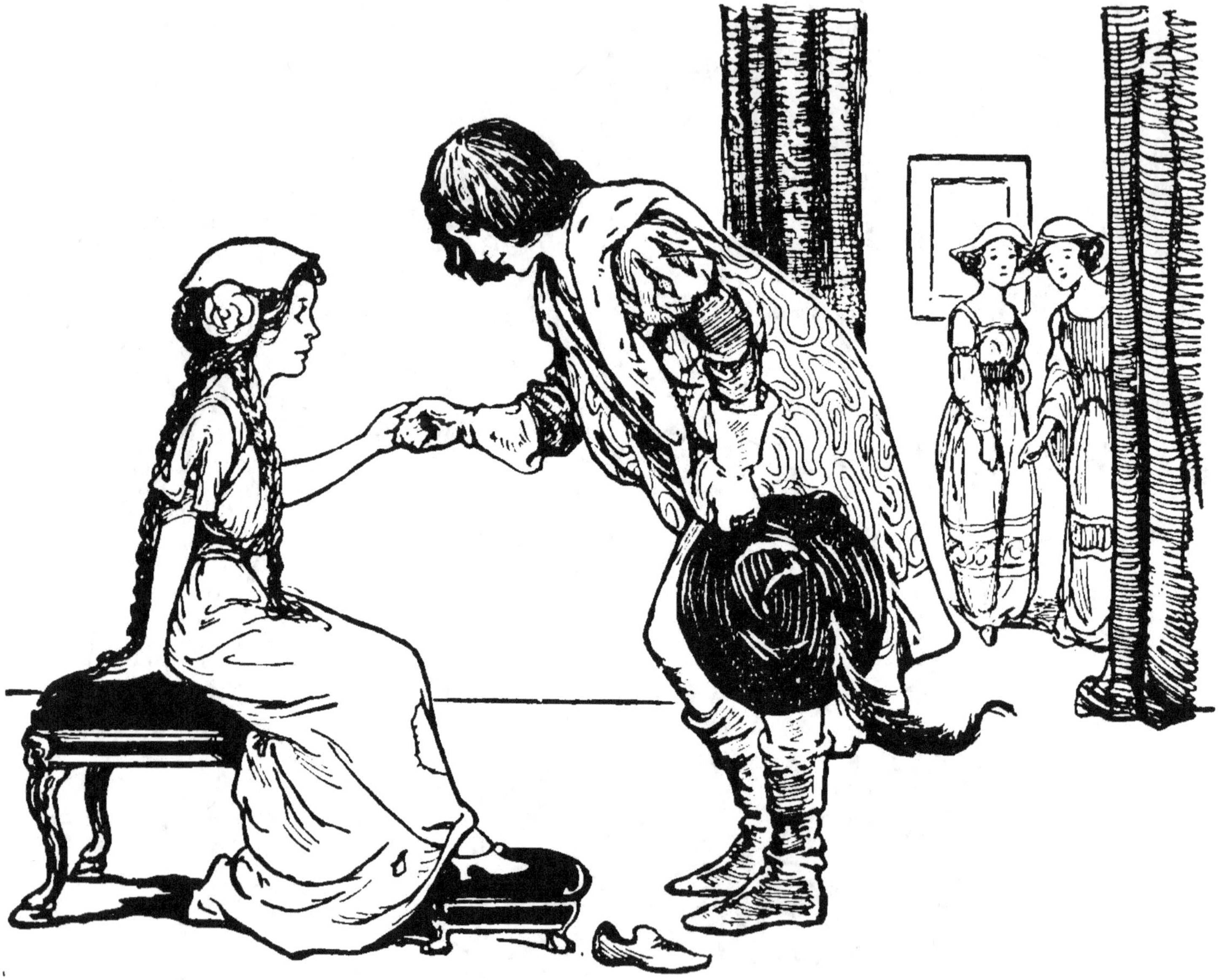

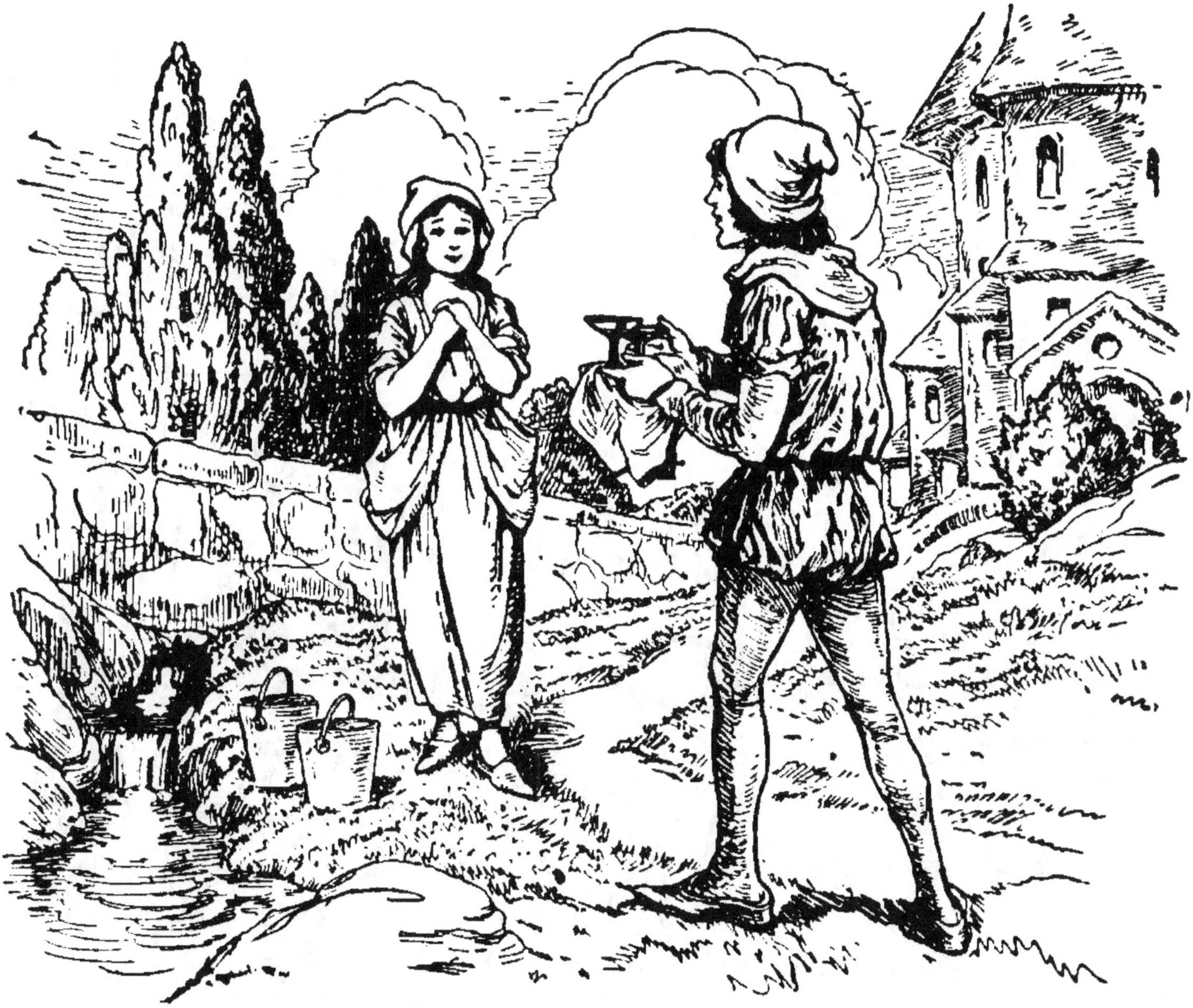

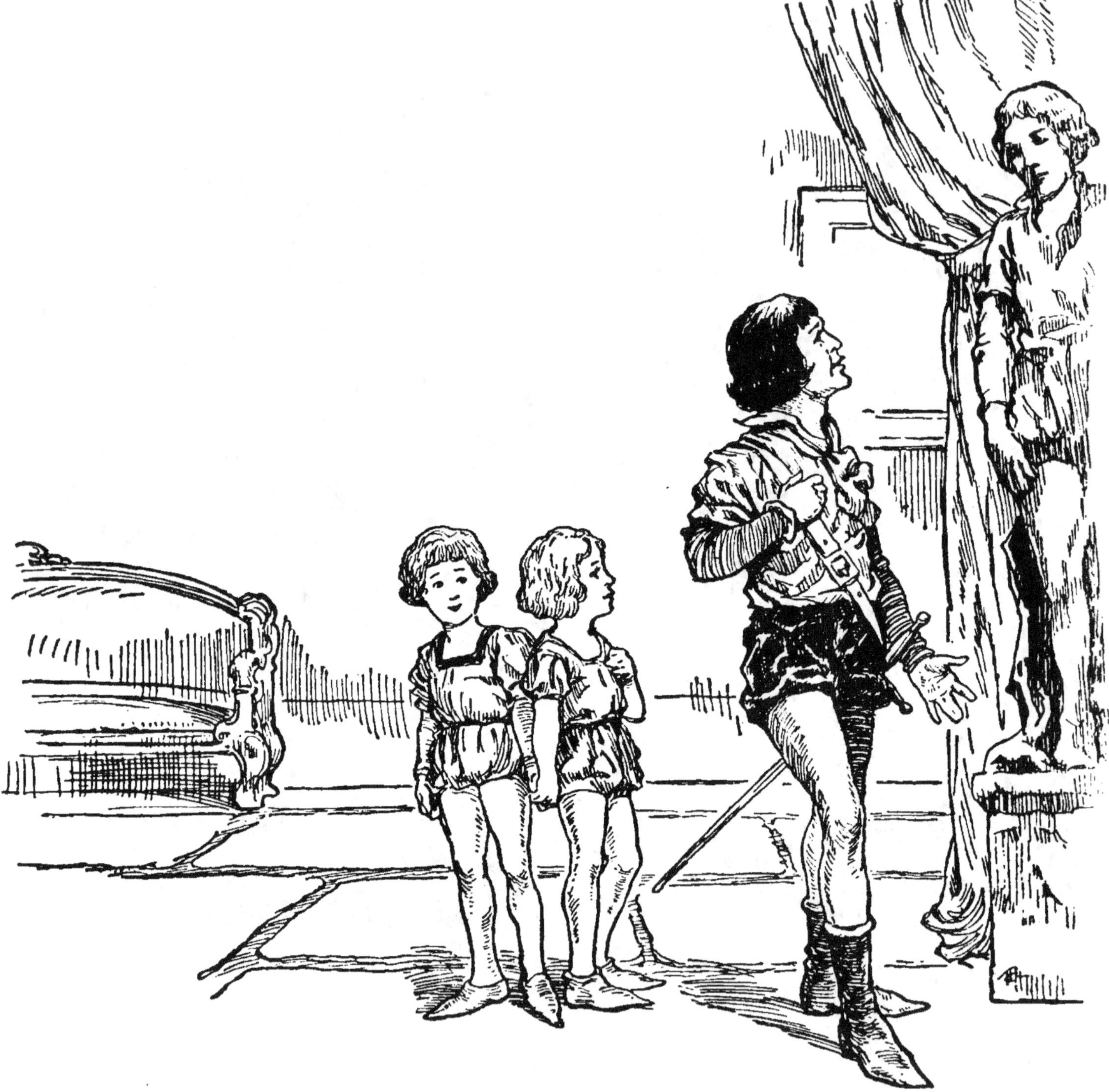

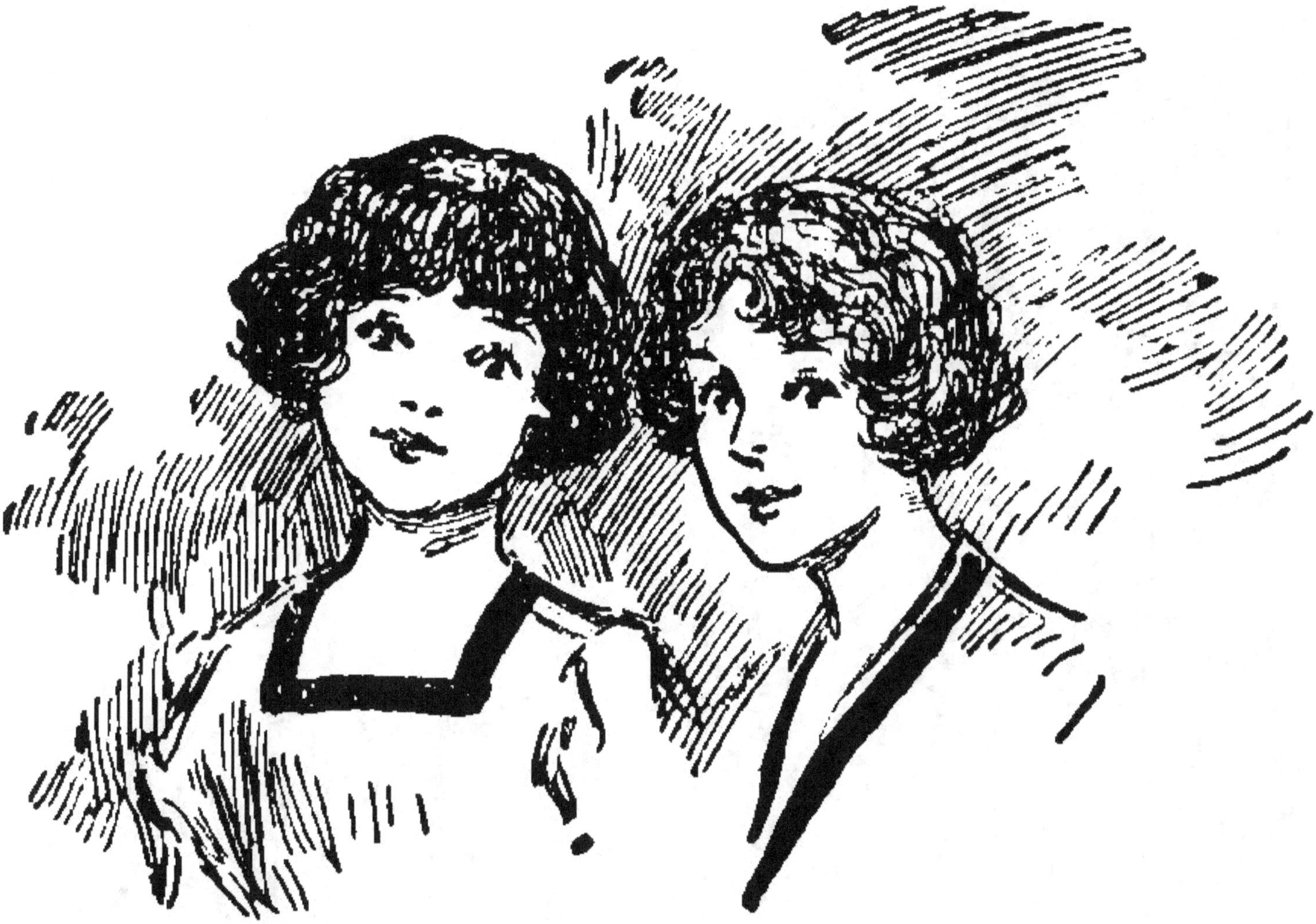

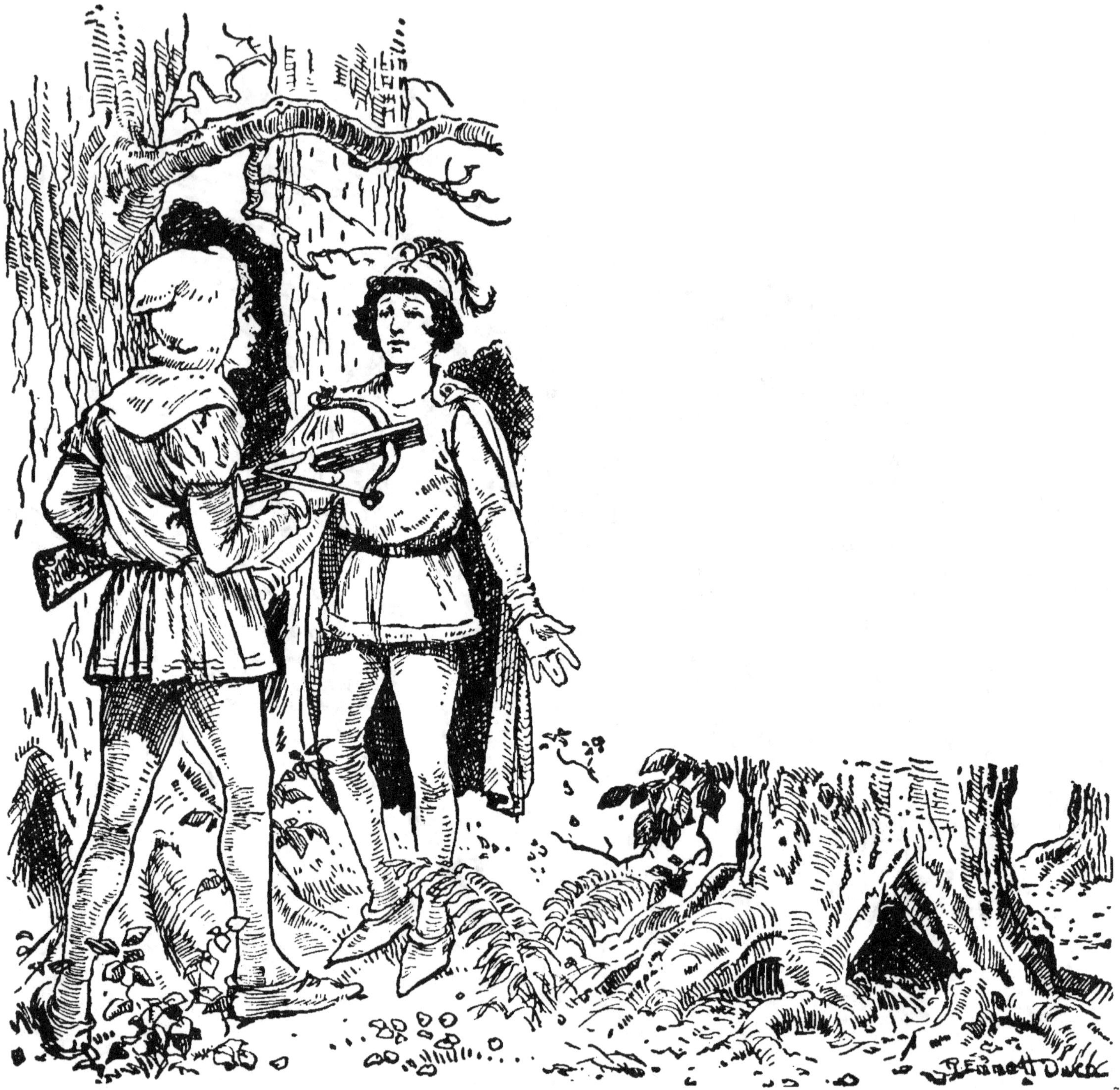

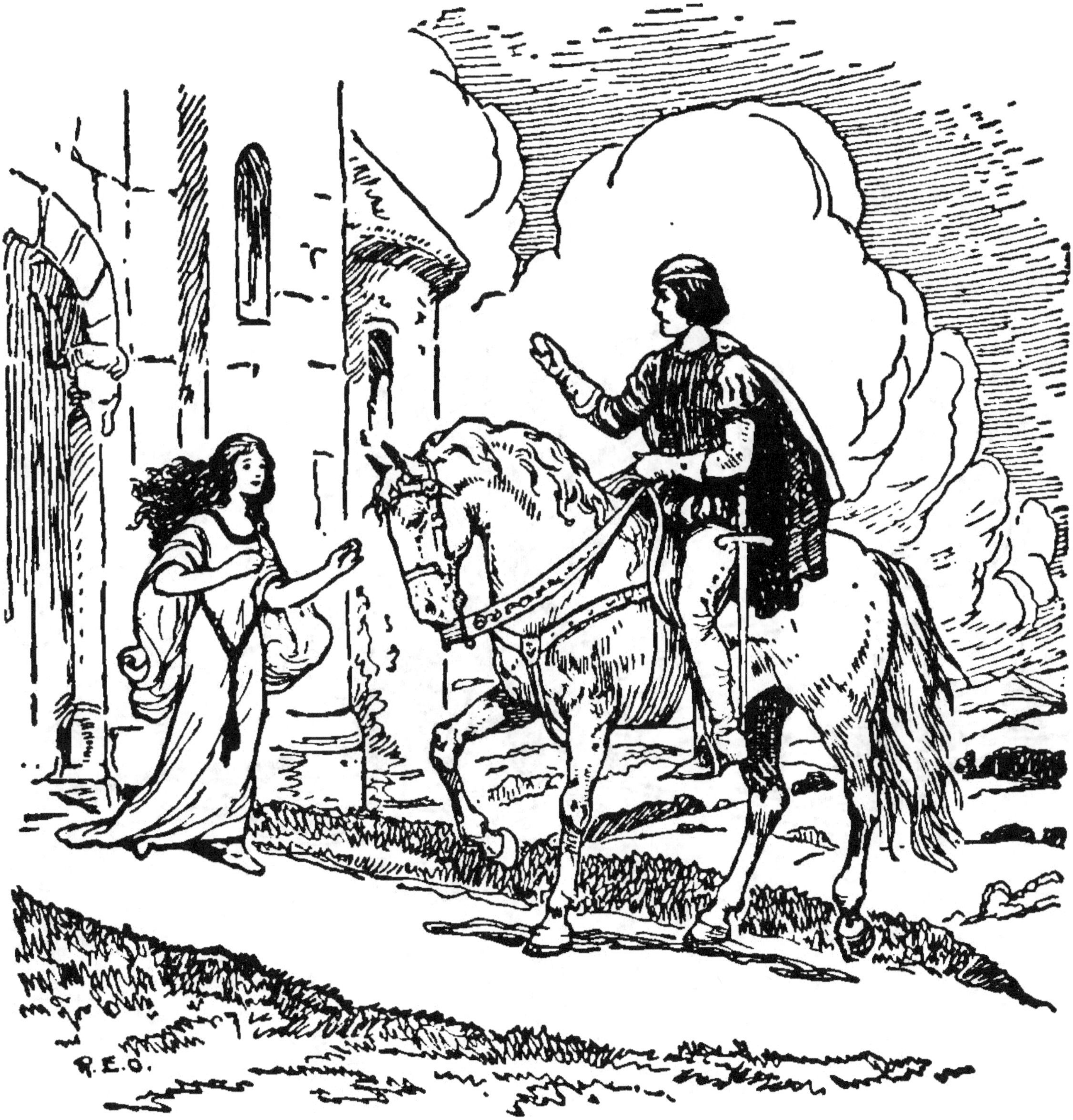
R.E.O.

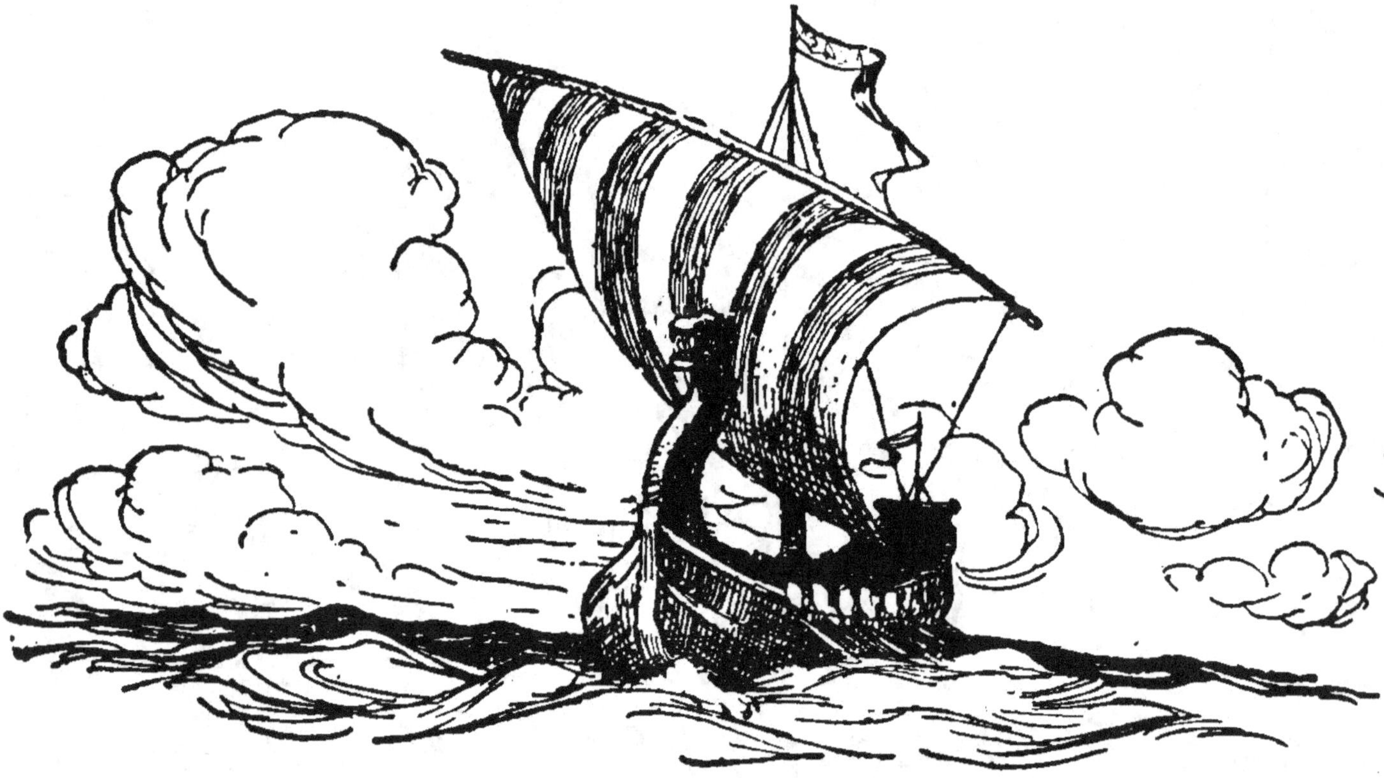

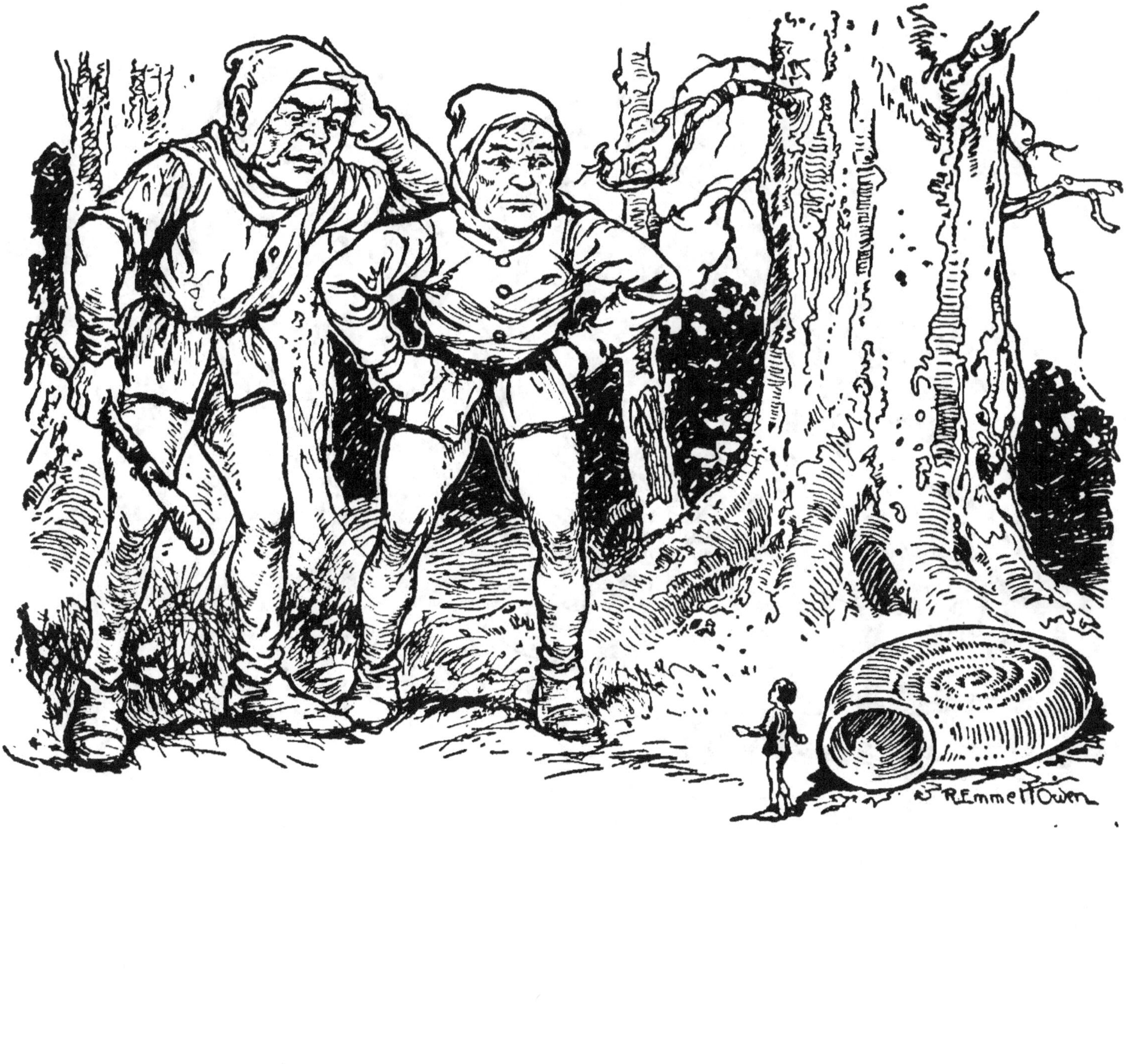
R.Emmett Owen

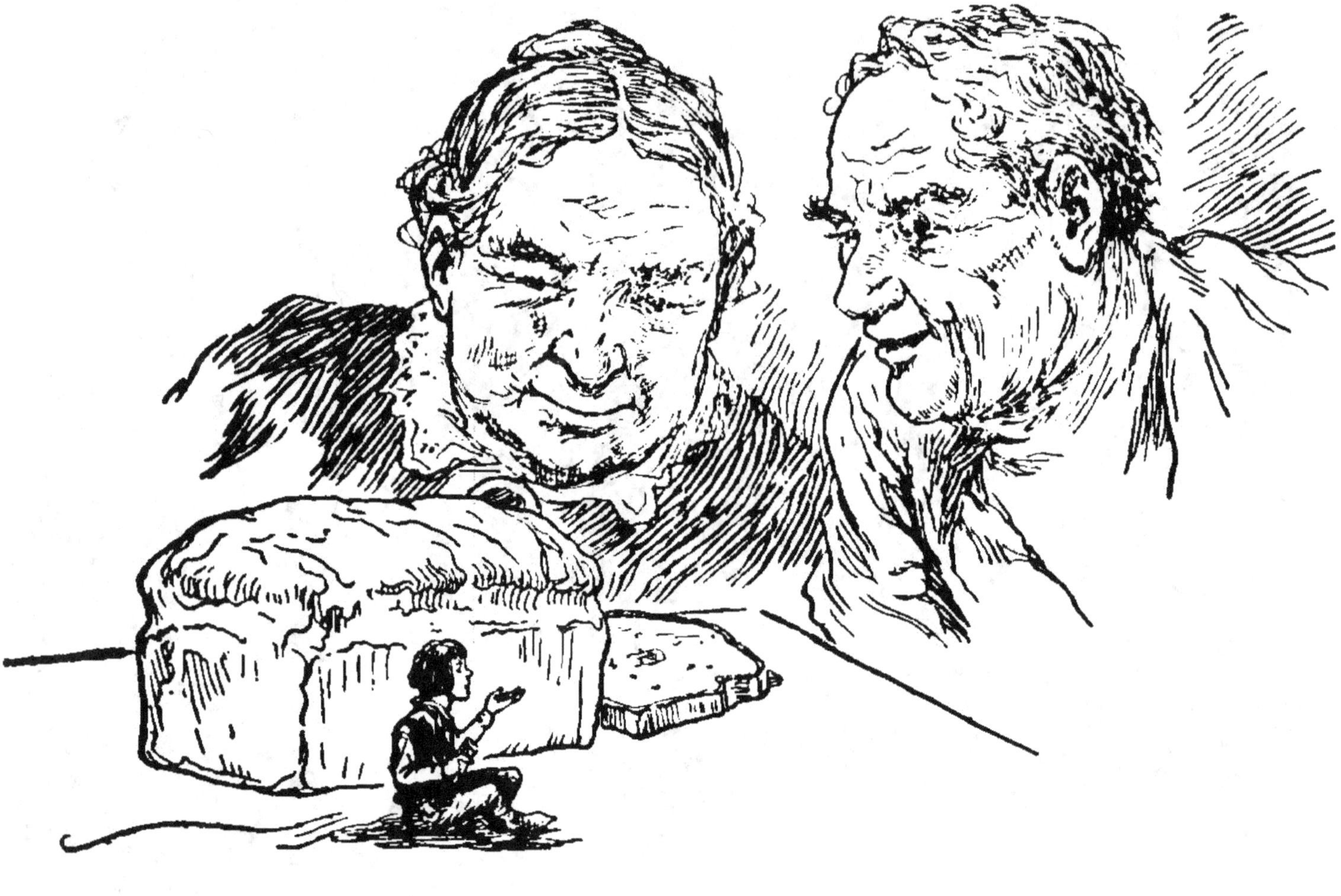

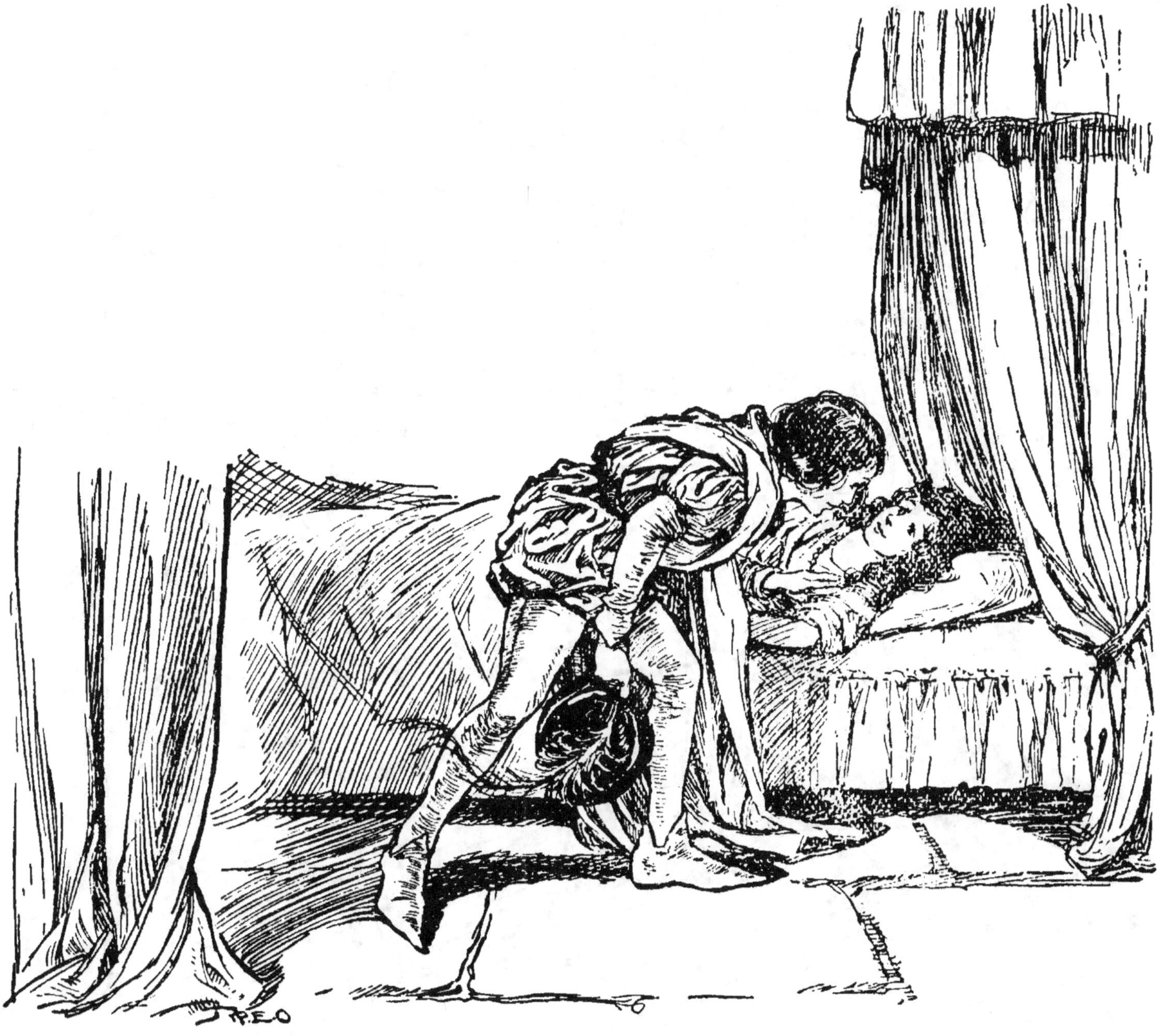

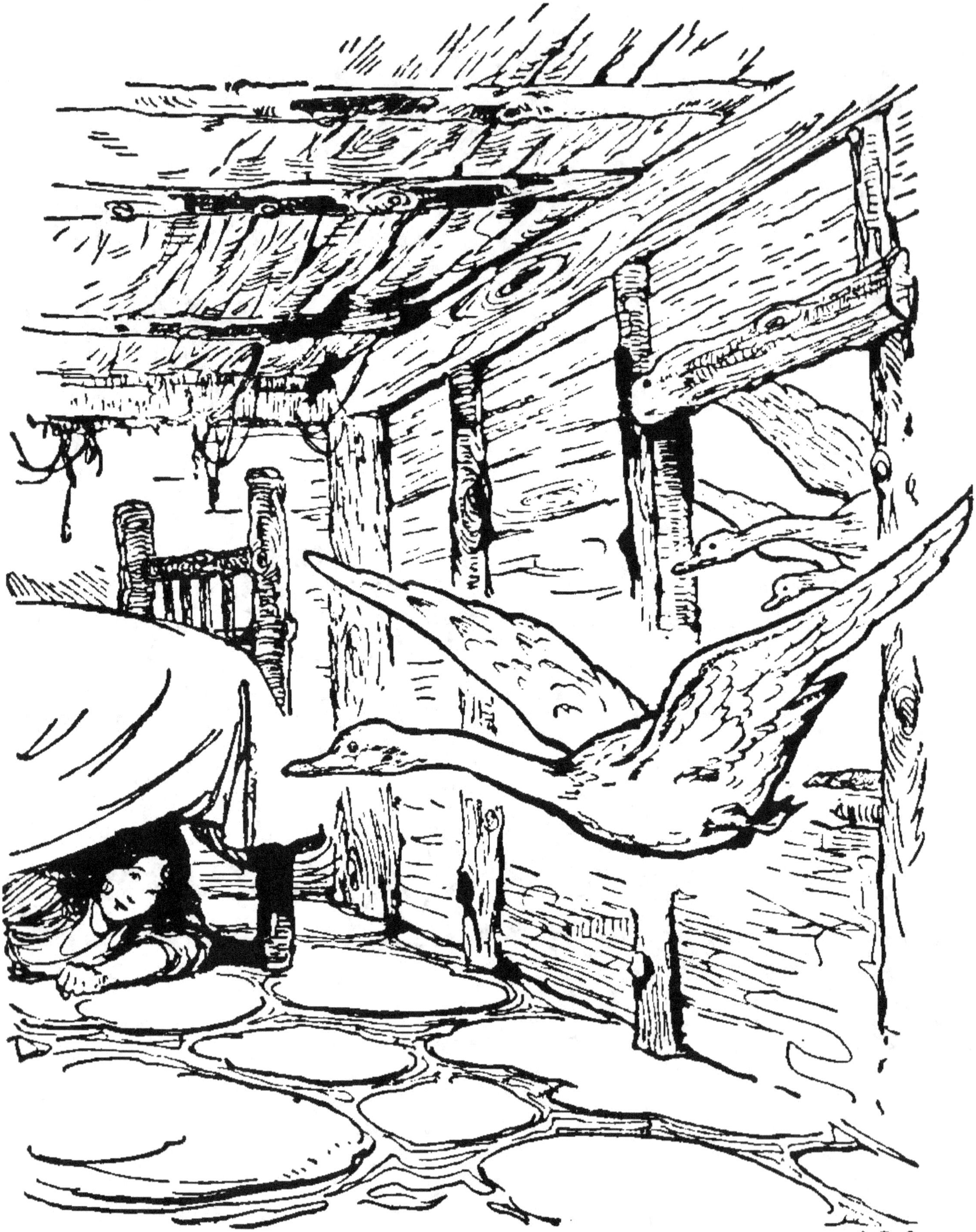

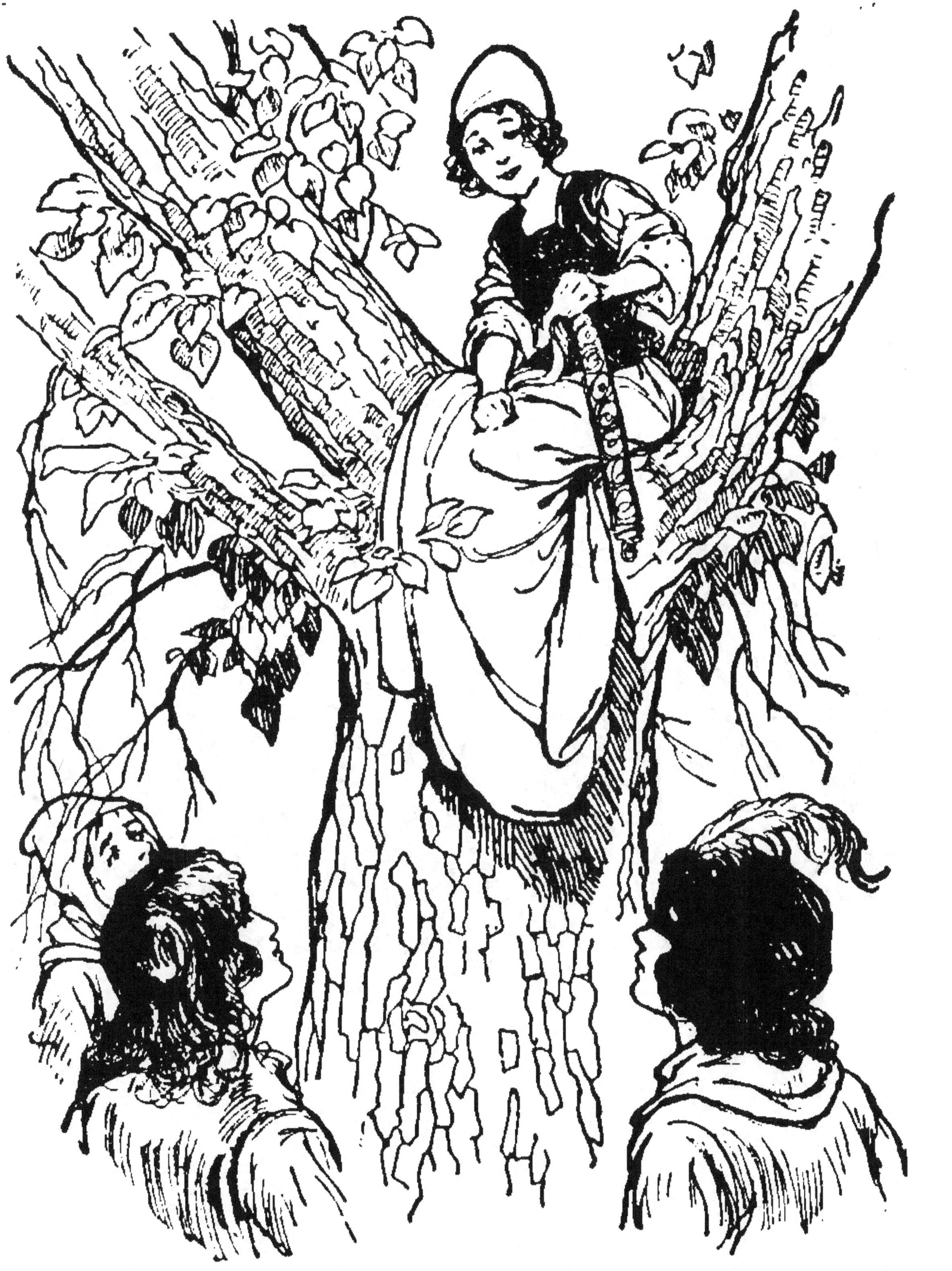

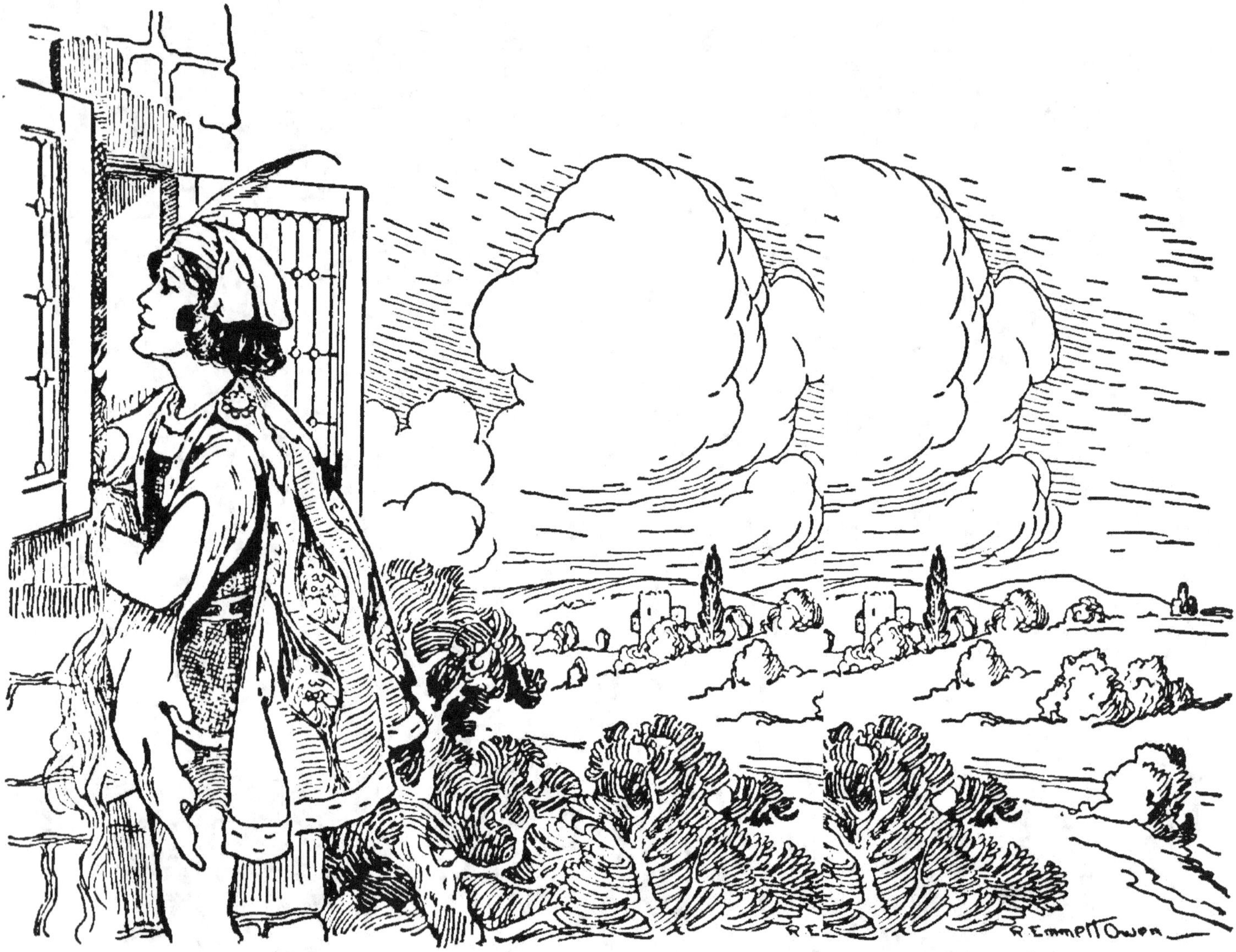
R Emmett Owen

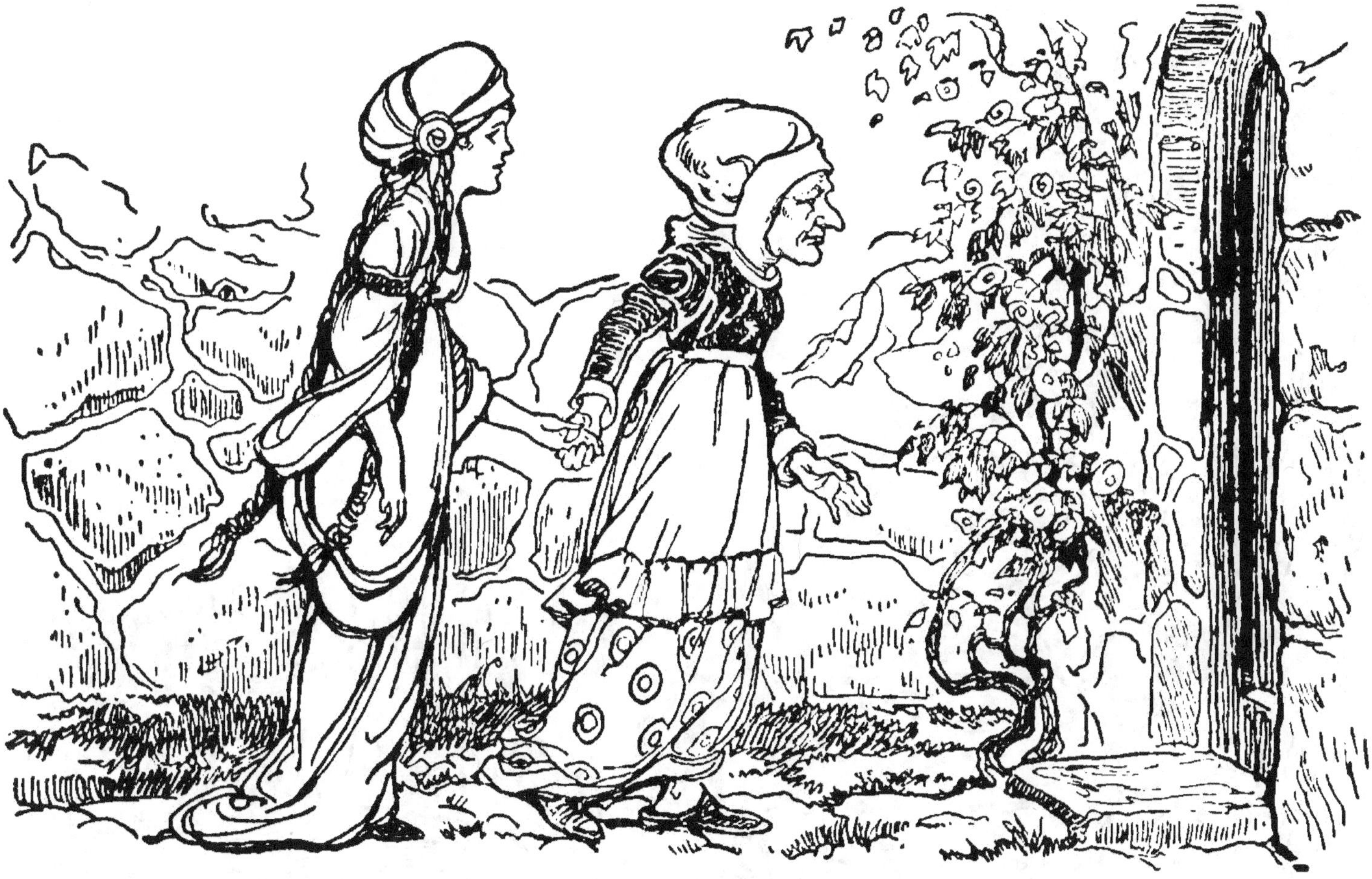

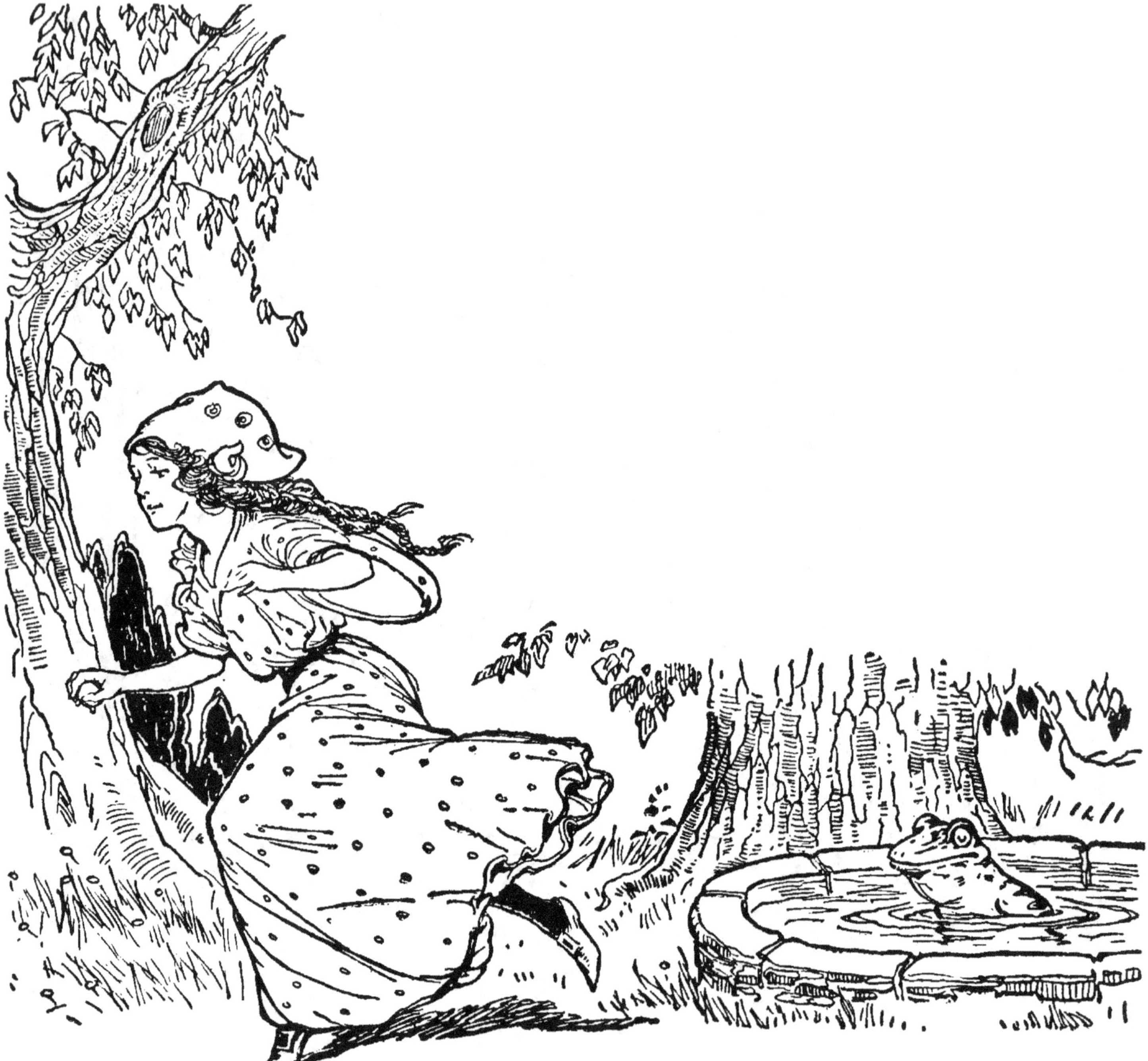

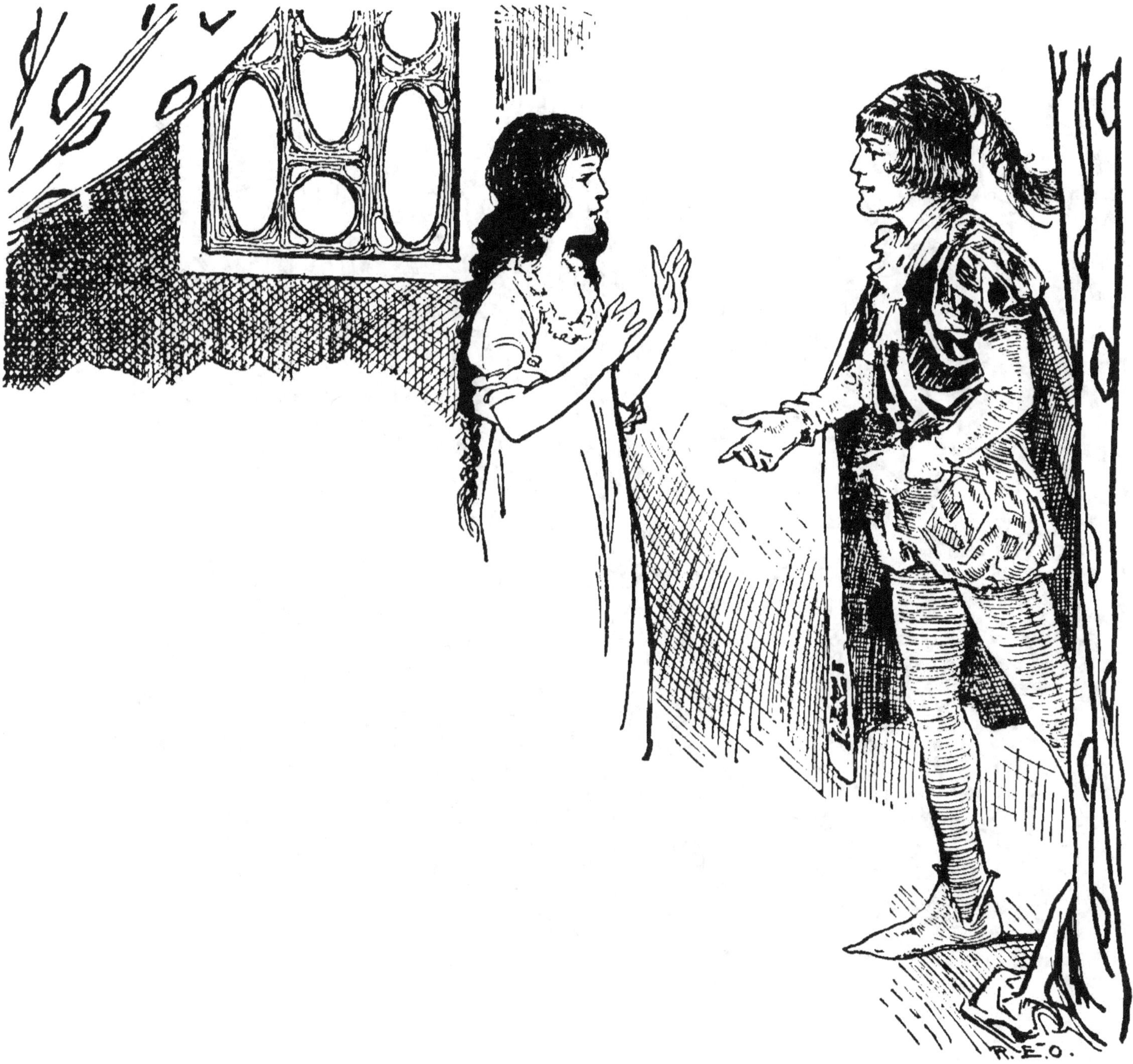
R. E. O.

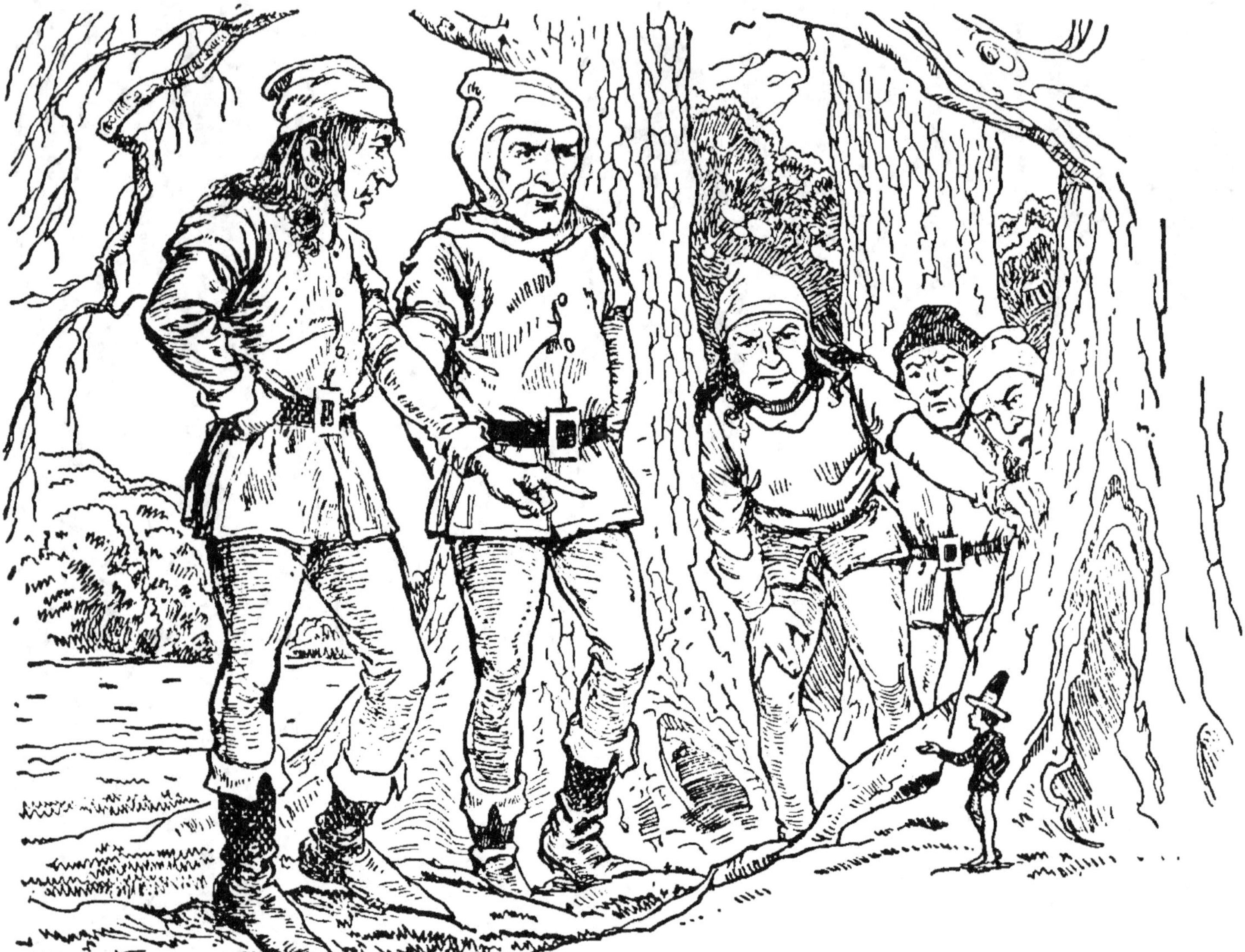
R.EmmettOwen

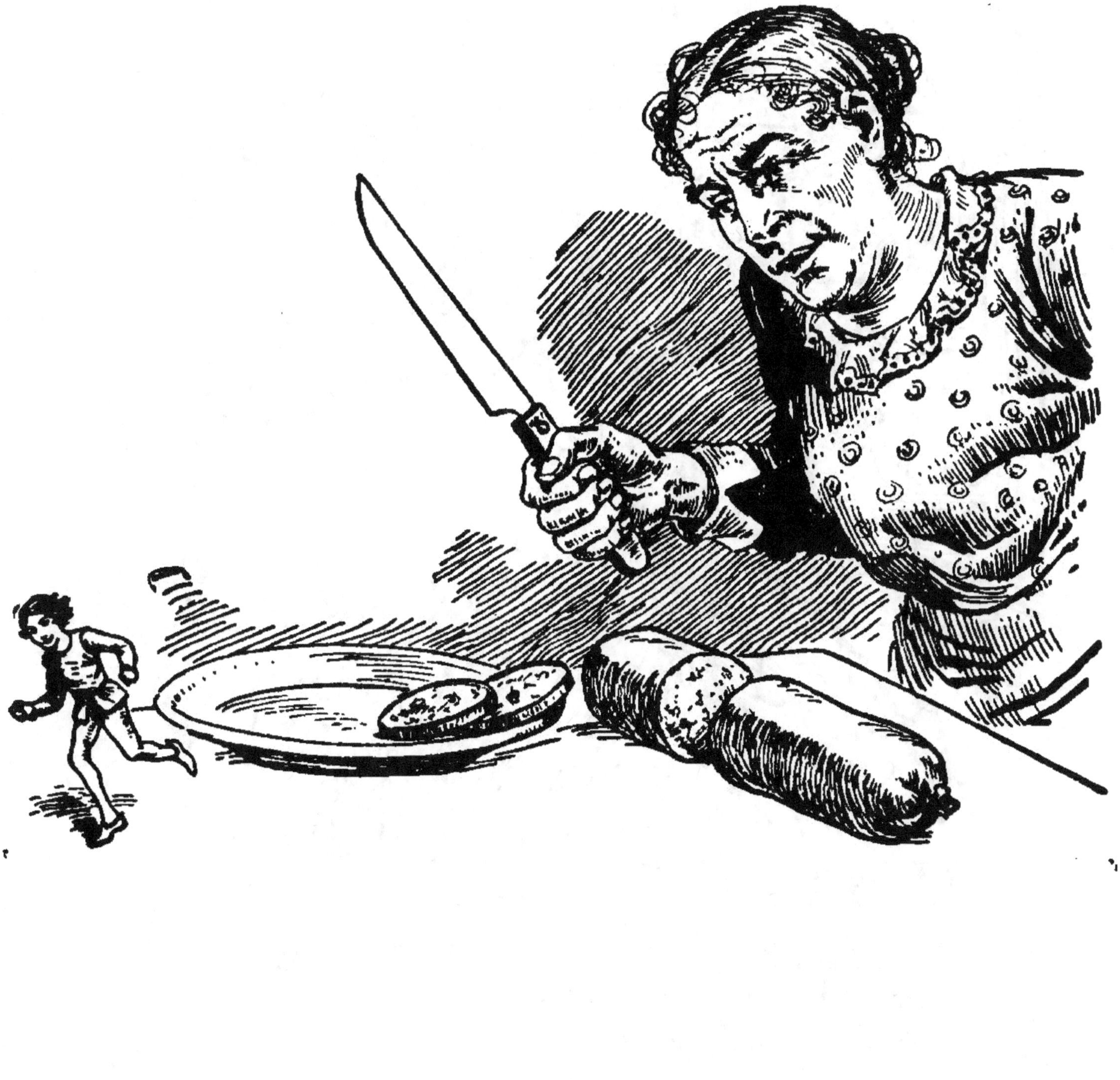

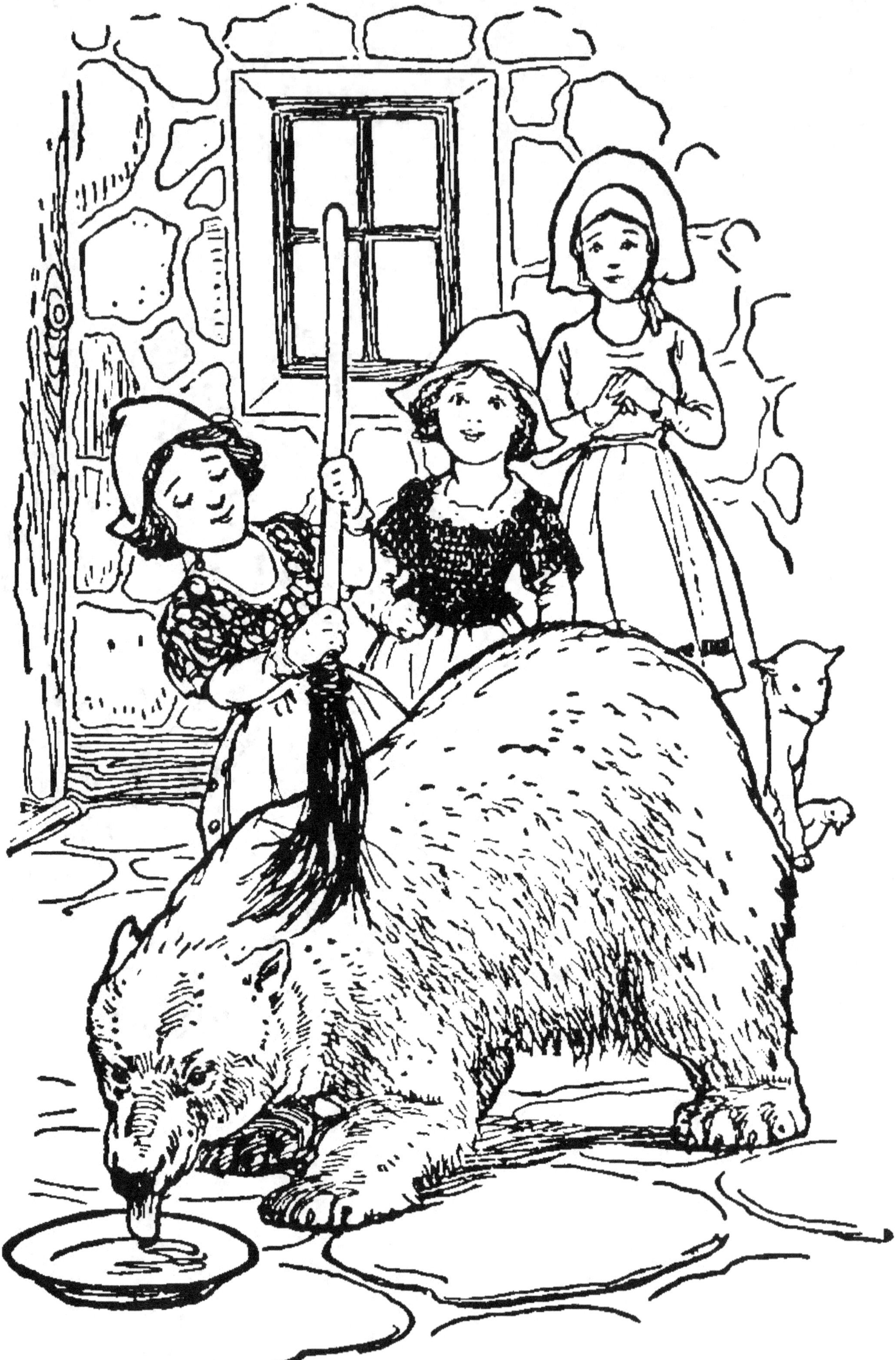

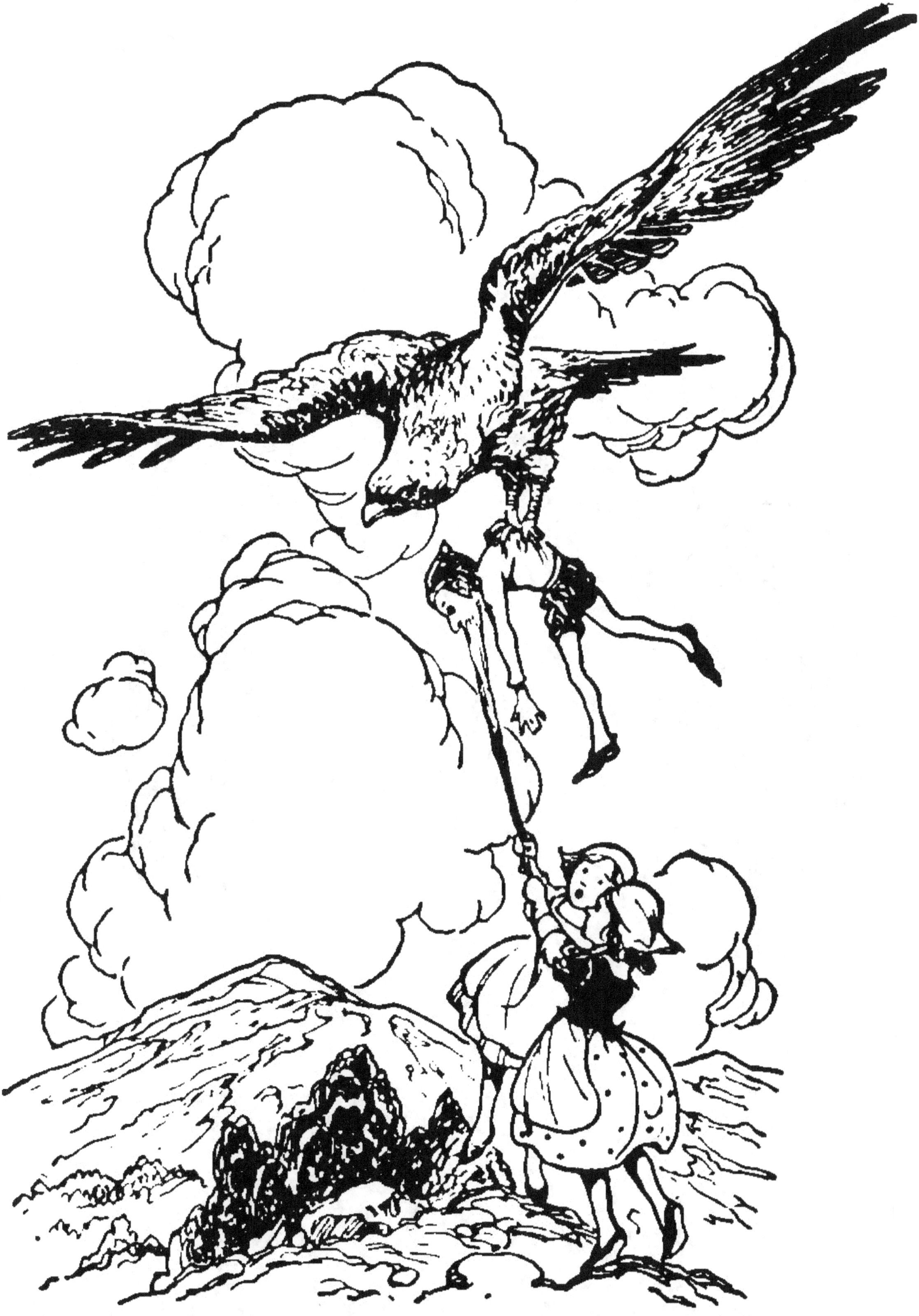

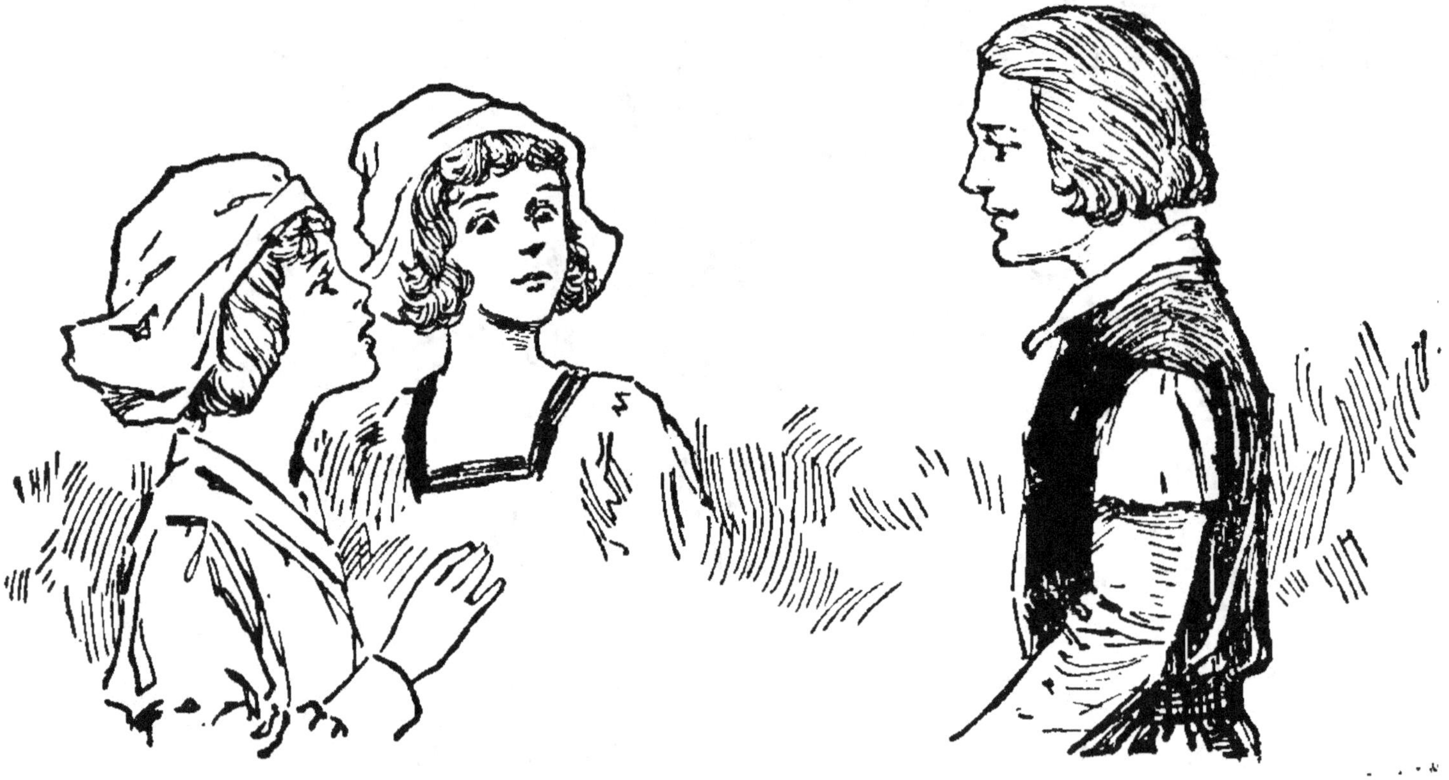

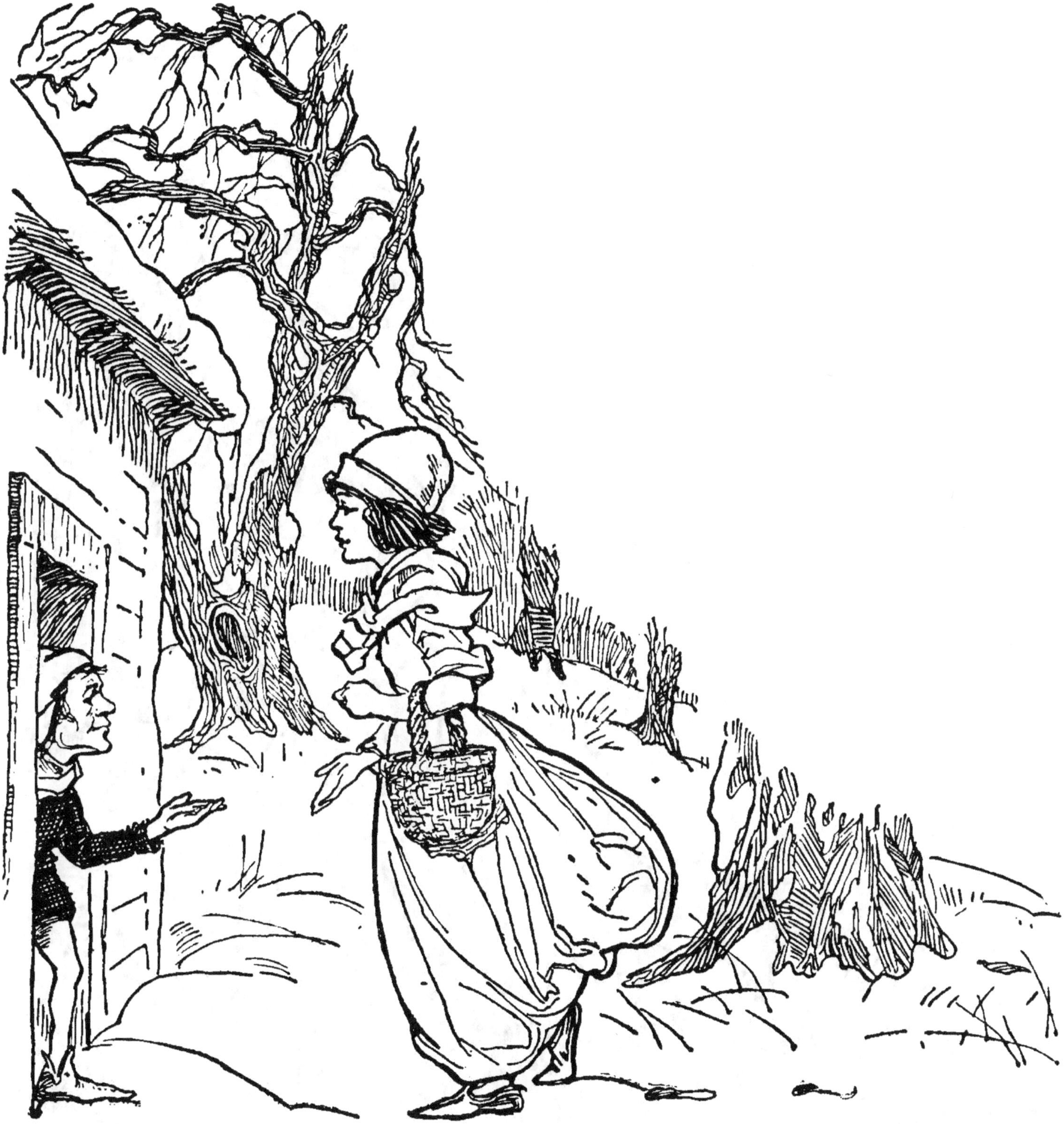

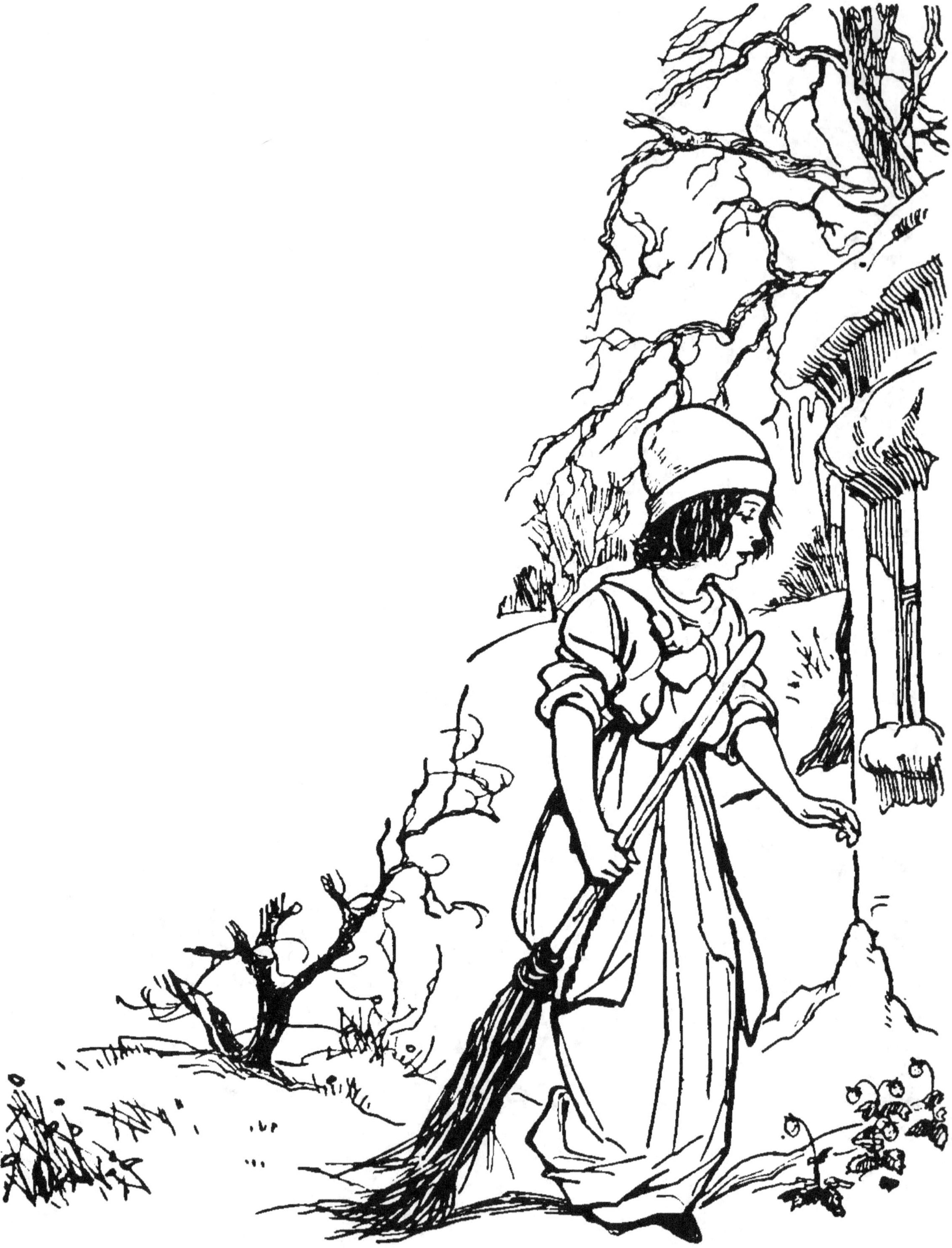

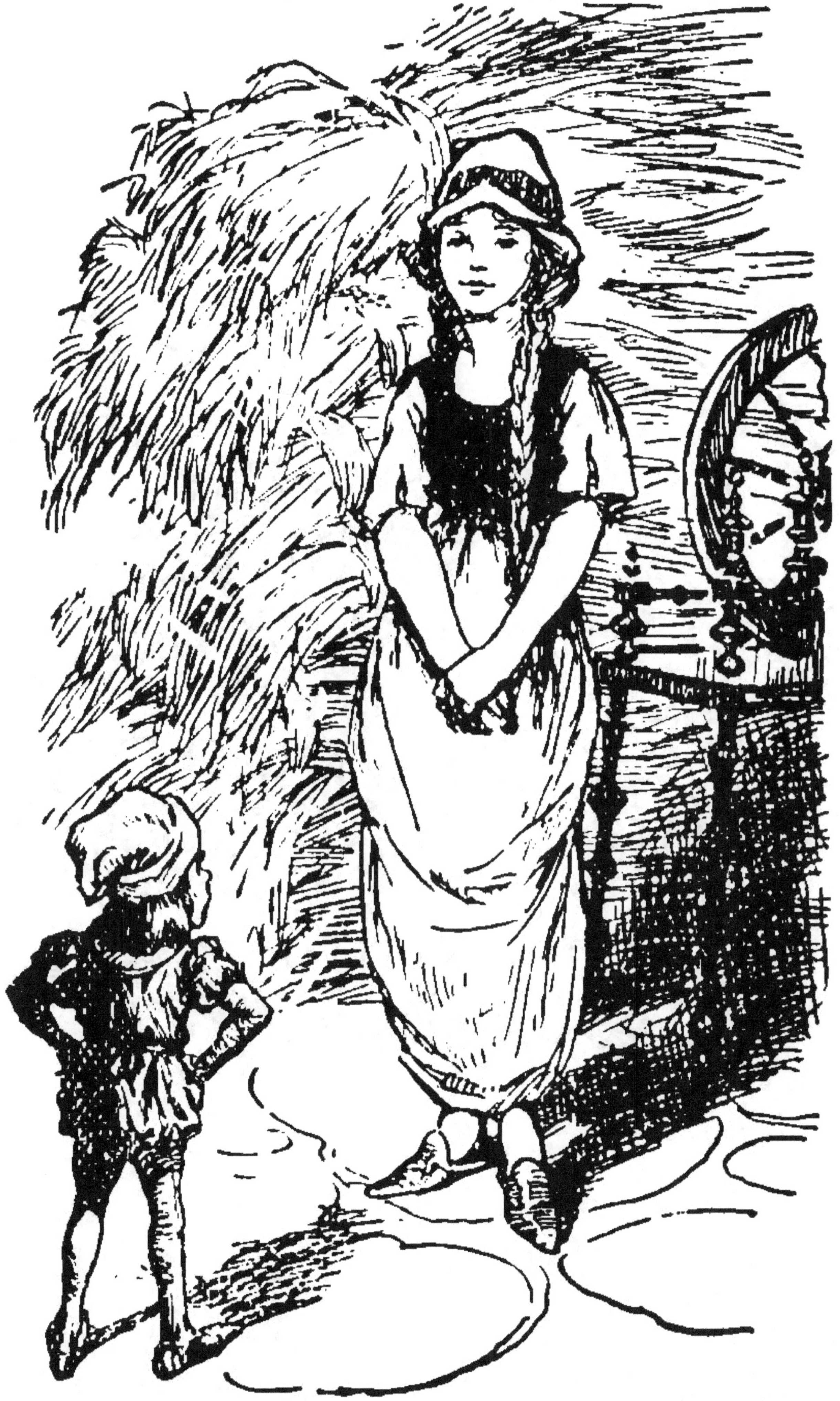

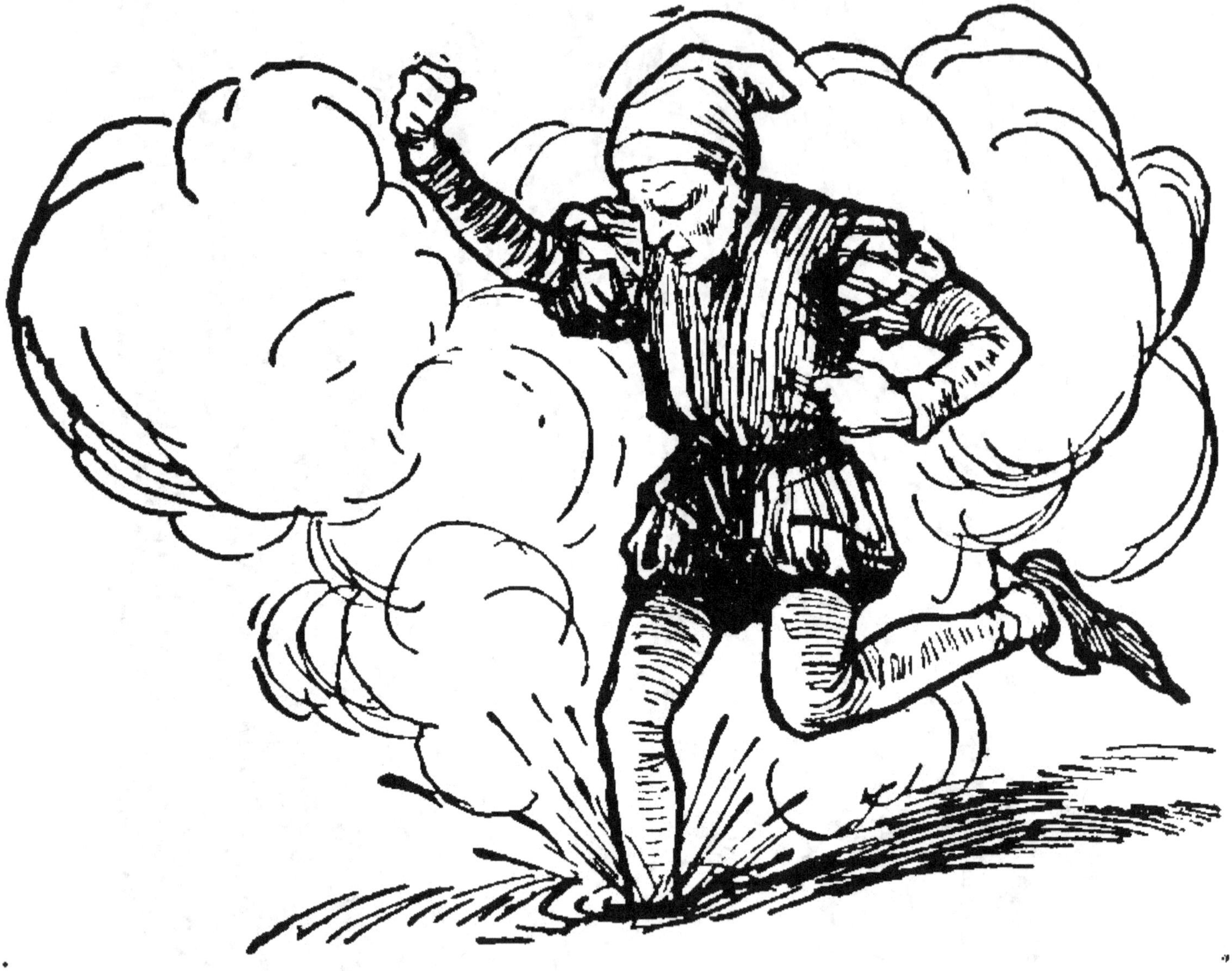

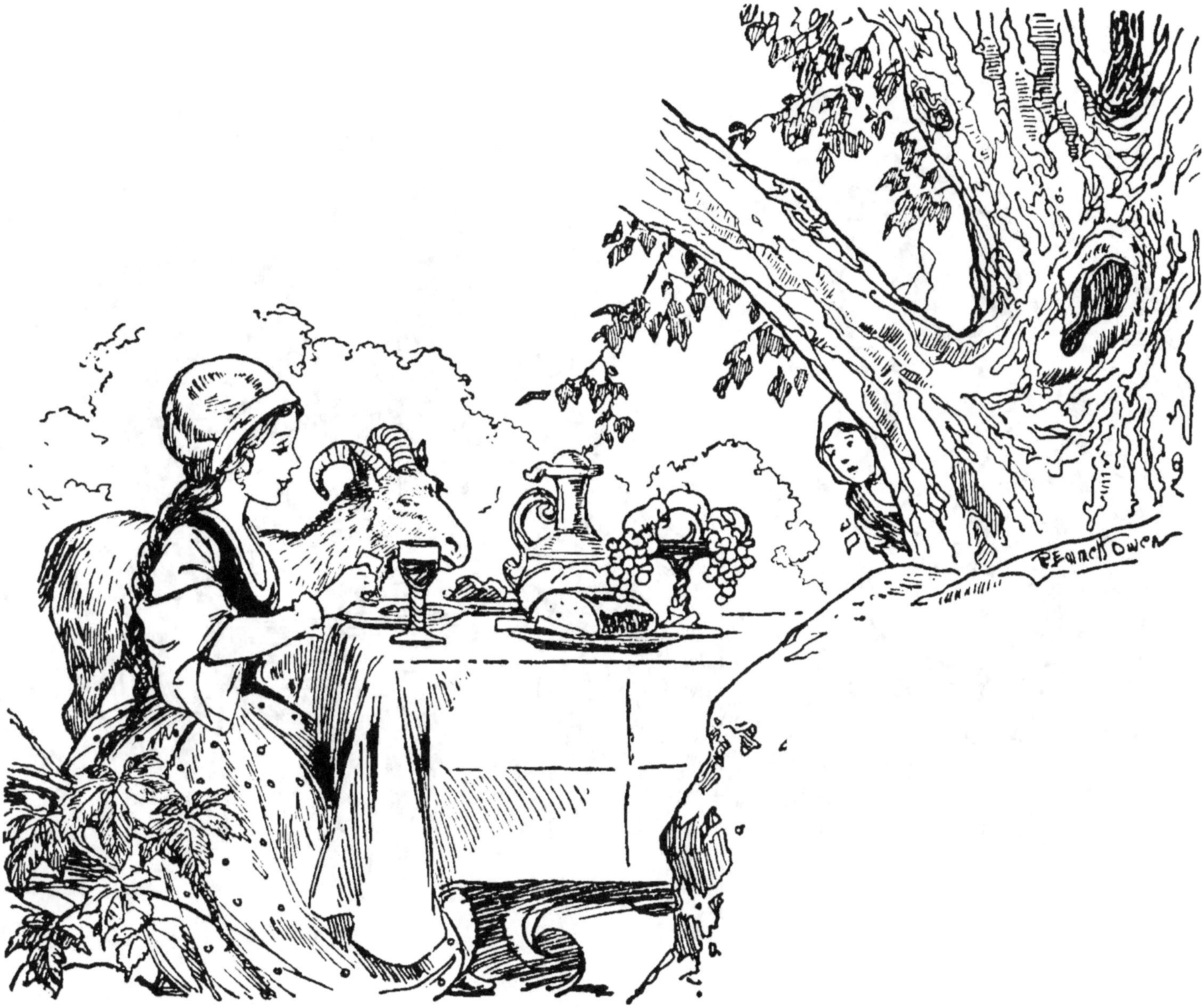

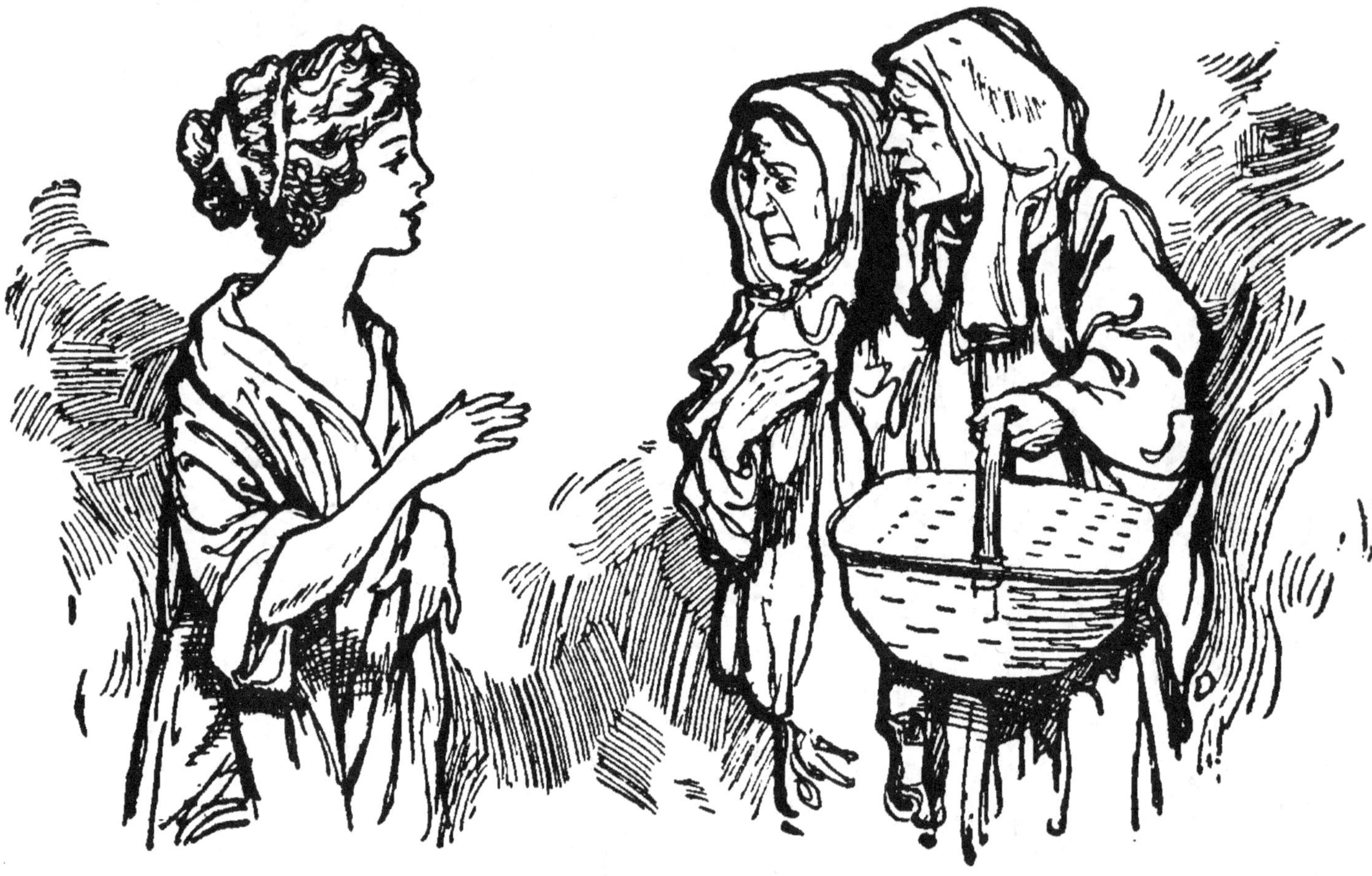

www.ingramcontent.com/pod-product-compliance
Lightning Source LLC
Chambersburg PA
CBHW082120220526
45472CB00009B/2252
9781719391597